FACING PANIC:

Self-Help for People with Panic Attacks

R. Reid Wilson, Ph.D.

Anxiety Disorders Association of America

About the Author
R. Reid Wilson, Ph.D. is Associate Clinical Professor of Psychiatry at the University of North Carolina School of Medicine in Chapel Hill, NC. He is the author of *Don't Panic: Taking Control of Anxiety Attacks* and co-author of *Stop Obsessing! How to Overcome Your Obsessions and Compulsions*. Dr. Wilson served on the Board of Directors of the Anxiety Disorders Association of America for 12 years and served as Program Chair of the ADAA's National Conference on Anxiety Disorders from 1988-1991. He is director of anxieties.com, a free self-help web site for sufferers of any of the anxiety disorders.

Disclaimer

This book contains general reference information and is not intended as a substitute for consulting with a physician or mental health care provider. Neither the publisher nor the author assumes any responsibility for any adverse effects that may result from your use of this book. Seek advice from your health care provider if, during the course of working with this book, you experience any new symptoms that you have not previously discussed.

FACING PANIC: SELF-HELP FOR PEOPLE WITH PANIC ATTACKS. Copyright © 2003 by R. Reid Wilson. All rights reserved. Printed in the United States of America.

The purchaser of this book has permission to make copies of Charts 1 through 7 for his or her personal use. Printable versions of the charts may be downloaded from the ADAA website at www.adaa.org. No other part of this book may be used or reproduced in any manner whatsoever without written permission except in the case of brief quotations embodied in critical articles and reviews. For information contact the Anxiety Disorders Association of America, 8730 Georgia Avenue, Suite 600, Silver Spring, MD 20910.

First Edition
ISBN 0-935943-01-3

About the ADAA

The Anxiety Disorders Association of America (ADAA) is the only national nonprofit organization of researchers, health care professionals, and individuals with anxiety disorders. The ADAA is dedicated to the early diagnosis, prevention and treatment of anxiety disorders. It is the Association's goal to promote professional and public awareness and understanding of these disorders. In addition, the ADAA seeks to increase the availability of effective treatment, reduce stigma, and stimulate research. To meet its mission, the ADAA is involved in a wide range of activities to educate professionals and the public about anxiety disorders. The ADAA holds an annual conference, sponsors an awards program to encourage young researchers and clinicians in the field, produces a newsletter, offers educational brochures on anxiety disorders and their treatments, and assists consumers in locating mental health professionals and self-help/support groups.

Anxiety disorders are real, serious and treatable. For more information about symptoms, diagnosis and treatment visit the ADAA website at www.adaa.org, or call the ADAA at 240-485-1001 for educational information.

For information about supporting the ADAA, please visit our website or call.

Anxiety Disorders Association of America
8730 Georgia Avenue, Suite 600
Silver Spring, MD 20910
(240) 485-1001
www.adaa.org

To Mary Bentha Wilson
and
Camille and Ginger Newman
Love Forever

Contents

Introduction   1

STEP 1: Recognize the Cycle of Your Panic   6
           The four common stages of panic   6
           Your two challenges: conditioning and
           catastrophic predictions   9
           Agoraphobia and the avoidance cycle   13
           Breaking free of the panic cycle   14

STEP 2: Learn about Conditioning and the Body's
           Special Emergency Response   15
           Summary   21

STEP 3: Practice the Calming Skills   23
           Calming your breath   24
           Quieting your body   25
           Tracking your practice   29
           A special note   30

STEP 4: Adopt a New Self-Help Strategy   31
           Get anxious on purpose   33
           Once you are anxious, encourage the
              symptoms to continue for a long time   35
           During this time, stop worrying and start
              supporting yourself   37
           Let go of your safety crutches   40
           Do this over and over, in all your fearful
              situations   46

STEP 5:	Purposely Create Your Symptoms	47
	How to practice	51
STEP 6:	Take Your Skills Out into Your World	59
	Planning for your practice	61
	Practicing your skills	62
	What to do if your physical sensations or worries become too uncomfortable for you	67
	After the Practice	68
STEP 7:	Now, Greet Panic in Your Daily Life	71
	Stop resisting panic	71
	Choice 1: Permit the symptoms	72
	Choice 2: Provoke your symptoms	76

Some Final Words   79

Acknowledgements

This book is a major revision of my original booklet, *Breaking the Panic Cycle: Self Help for People with Phobias*, published by the ADAA in 1987. The changes here are significant enough that I have modified the title to reflect the new orientation toward self-help for panic attacks. Several new and innovative approaches are being introduced in this revision.

Some might think that I have developed this book from my own creativity and skill. I have not. *Facing Panic: Self-Help for People with Panic Attacks* reflects the work of hundreds of innovative researchers and clinicians in the field of anxiety. I offer my gratitude and appreciation for their tireless efforts and intelligent inventiveness. Their dedication to the field has allowed me to pass on to you the most efficient and direct approaches for conquering panic that we know today.

There are particular researchers and clinicians whom I would like to thank for their contributions to the field. Please understand that for every individual I name, there are six or seven others who deserve honor for their roles in furthering this work. David Barlow, Ph.D. has done groundbreaking work for decades, and Michelle Craske, Ph.D. joined him in innovating interoceptive exposure, introduced here in Step 5. David M. Clark, D. Phil. has cleverly designed studies to further the techniques and theories of brief cognitive therapy. Wolfgang Fiegenbaum, Dipl. Psych. and colleagues highlighted the importance of internal sensations as sources of anxiety and fear. Edna Foa, Ph.D. and Michael Kozak, Ph.D. generated core principles for how to modify fear. David Spiegel, M.D., Stefan Hoffmann, Ph.D. and Nina Heinrichs, Dipl. Psych. are studying the essential features of rapid, intense treatment of agoraphobia. Adrian Wells, Ph.D. and colleagues first identified safety behaviors used by socially anxious individuals, introduced here in Step 4 as "safety crutches." I would also like to thank Michael Otto, Ph.D. and Alec Pollard, Ph.D. for their expert advice on some important conceptual decisions in this book.

"When spider webs unite, they can tie up a lion." – Ethiopian proverb

Introduction

Are you suffering from panic attacks – anxiety attacks – or know someone who is? Panic attacks occur when people suddenly experience strong physical sensations coupled with frightening thoughts of losing control of their body, mind or current circumstances. Feeling this way can be a terrifying experience. If they reoccur for several weeks, these feelings can shape into a pattern. You may begin to fear the onset or return of the symptoms, then, after awhile, you find yourself in a state of high anxiety. Now you are even more convinced that a bout of panic is likely and you feel even more frightened of the future. So, you begin to avoid situations that might bring on a panic attack and the worry that it will be followed by another wave. This is called a panic cycle.

In this book, you will learn about the panic cycle and the many ways you can break it to regain control of your life. You will learn how to use the most up-to-date and effective self-help techniques, researched and put into use by experts from around the world. I will guide you each step of the way, offering advice and directions. Breaking free of the panic cycle is not complicated, but it is hard work. You will need a strong determination to overcome the symptoms of fear and avoidance. So, gather support around you, pull together your courage, and begin to see how you can take back control of your life.

Before and during an anxiety attack, people have frightening thoughts about bad things that might happen. I have listed some of those thoughts in Table 1. Which ones seem familiar to you?

> **TABLE 1: FEARED OUTCOMES DURING A PANIC ATTACK**
>
> - Fainting or collapsing in public
> - Losing control of your body
> - Becoming confused
> - Having a heart attack or other physical illness
> - Dying
> - Being trapped
> - Causing a scene
> - Going crazy
> - Being unable to breathe
> - Being unable to get home or to another "safe place"

Persistent panic attacks are commonly related to a psychological problem called panic disorder. But they also occur in other disorders. Table 2, on the following page, briefly characterizes several such disorders.

The symptoms of panic may be a reaction to a number of physical problems. For example, a person with a chronic obstructive lung disease, such as emphysema, might begin to panic whenever he or she experiences a shortness of breath. Someone recovering from a heart attack might panic when noticing mild discomfort in the chest. These anxious responses may seem like reasonable reactions to stressful situations. But, in the years to come, researchers may also discover that some people are genetically predisposed to panic while others are not, or are less prone to it. The nervous systems and psychological makeup of some people are simply more sensitive to the stresses of life for genetic reasons.

Just as several physical disorders can produce symptoms mimicking those of a panic attack, such as dizziness, racing heart or difficulty breathing, there are medications with side effects that can cause similar responses. This means that it is important that you see your personal physician before beginning any self-help program for panic. You should be sure there are no physical problems contributing to your symptoms. If, while practicing any skills in this book, you experience new symptoms that concern you, consult your physician.

TABLE 2: PANIC WITHIN PSYCHOLOGICAL DISORDERS

PANIC DISORDER — This is the only psychological condition whose primary pattern of symptoms is recurring panic attacks. Initially, these feelings come unexpectedly. As the cycle progresses, the person fears more attacks and may avoid places where they previously had an attack.

PANIC DISORDER WITH AGORAPHOBIA — People with panic disorder may also develop agoraphobia. They may significantly limit their lifestyle due to a strong fear coupled with a strong desire to avert panic. They avoid such situations as enclosed spaces (stores, restaurants), travel (cars, bridges, planes), open spaces (wide streets, fields), confinement or restriction of movement (hairdresser's or dentist's chair, lines, crowds), or being alone.

SPECIFIC PHOBIA — A phobia is an intense fear of a particular object or situation that poses little or no actual danger. The person may either completely avoid the situation or approach it with great anxiety. The most common phobias are of specific animals and insects, fears of nature (storms, water), heights and closed-in spaces. The person may have a panic attack when confronting these situations.

SOCIAL ANXIETY DISORDER (SOCIAL PHOBIA) — People with social anxiety disorder worry that they will embarrass themselves in front of others. These circumstances include public speaking, urinating in public bathrooms, signing one's name, and being watched while eating. A sense of panic occurs when he or she becomes involved in these situations.

POSTTRAUMATIC STRESS DISORDER — PTSD is a specific emotional distress that can follow a major psychologically traumatic event, such as a rape or assault, a natural disaster, a serious accident, major surgery, or combat. Symptoms may include nightmares or flashbacks of the event, avoiding any situations that remind the person of the trauma, and an emotional numbing of feelings in connection with it. Panic attacks may be part of this constellation of symptoms.

OBSESSIVE-COMPULSIVE DISORDER — OCD involves persistent negative thoughts (obsessions) that are involuntary, uncontrollable, and consuming. The person may also repeat actions or thoughts (rituals, or compulsions) that seem to help them reduce the anxiety. Still, panic may take over when the individual attempts to stop the obsessions or rituals.

GENERALIZED ANXIETY DISORDER — GAD occurs as a non-specific form of anxiety and worry concerning such topics as family, money, work, or health, even when they involve seemingly minor problems. Occasionally, the degree of concern leads one to experience an anxiety attack.

How to use this book.

In this book, I will guide you through seven self-help steps to breaking the cycle of panic. It may be a good idea for you to read the entire book and then return to study each step in more detail. As I said before, you will need determination.

While I have organized the book into seven steps, you also have two basic tasks. You will notice, starting in Step 3, that I ask you to practice exercises in order to develop the skills you will need. Be sure to set aside several times during the week when you can do this. There are charts to fill out, activities to complete, and checklists to check. Full-size versions of the charts may be downloaded from the ADAA website, www.adaa.org. Your second task is just as important: to challenge your beliefs, to re-think your viewpoint about how to manage your symptoms and your fears. Reading these pages without practicing any of the skills may turn out to be a powerful reminder of how hard it is for you to take back control of your life. In the same way, if you go through the exercises without adopting a new attitude toward conquering your panic, you may feel frustrated and disappointed.

So do both! I will point out these new stances toward panic and repeat them a number of times throughout these pages. By understanding these principles, and applying them through the structured exercises, you will be building your confidence and your skills based on a solid foundation.

Here are the seven steps:

STEP 1: Recognize the Cycle of Your Panic
STEP 2: Learn about Conditioning and the Body's Special Emergency Response
STEP 3: Practice the Calming Skills
STEP 4: Adopt a New Self-Help Strategy
Get anxious on purpose.
Once you are anxious, encourage the symptoms to continue for a long time.
During this time, stop worrying and start supporting yourself.
Let go of your safety crutches.
Do this over and over, in all your fearful situations.
STEP 5: Purposely Create Your Symptoms
STEP 6: Take Your Skills Out into Your World
STEP 7: Now, Greet Panic in Your Daily Life

STEP 1: Recognize the Cycle of Your Panic

The first panic attack—with its physical symptoms of a racing heart, sweaty palms, dry mouth, and rapid breathing—might come from out-of-the-blue. Or, it might be a reaction to an anxiety-provoking situation such as the beginning of a speech you are about to deliver, or being trapped briefly in an elevator, or feeling the pressure of a deadline. Initially, you might shrug off the experience either as a random event or the normal tensions of your busy day. Why? Because for most people panic is a rare occurrence.

The Four Common Stages of Panic
But if you continue to encounter episodes of seemingly overwhelming panic your reactions may begin to change. Over time, you may experience what we will call the cycle of panic, like the pattern illustrated in Graph 1.

Since an attack can be so traumatic – some people feel as though they are dying – your mind easily recalls the memory of that experience. Simply thinking of venturing near that same situation again can produce anxious, fearful thoughts. The more time you spend anticipating that upcoming event, the more frightened you become.

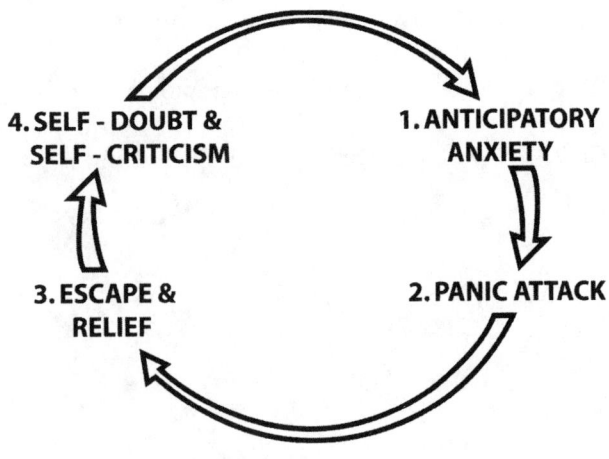

Graph 1: The Cycle of Panic

This is because the human body reacts to events based on our interpretation of those events and the predictions we derive from them. For example, you may tell yourself, "I will soon enter a crowded store. I have had a panic attack in stores before. I'm not certain I can manage walking through this one." Physically, you will become more tense and guarded in response to those thoughts. And, as you become aware of the growing physical sensations, you become more worried. Your next thought might be, "It feels as though I'm beginning to panic now." In effect, these anxious thoughts and physical sensations begin the first stage of the panic cycle. We call this stage *Anticipatory Anxiety*, the worry and physical tension you feel as you approach a threatening situation.

The *Panic Attack* itself is the traumatic second stage in this cycle.

During a panic attack, one of the strongest messages people send themselves is the urge to flee. "I have to get out of here." Escape from that panic-provoking situation seems to be your only choice. By leaving the scene, one usually does feel relief. The body slowly returns to normalcy. The heart rate slows. Breathing returns to normal. You stop feeling shaky or dizzy. At the same time, you tell yourself, "Thank goodness I left!" Stage three of the panic cycle is the state of *Escape and Relief*.

However, as Graph 2 illustrates, escaping the anxious scene will actually reinforce the cycle of panic. To understand how this works, let's break down the major behavioral components that make up this special escape scenario. Imagine that you fear having a panic attack while driving your car on an interstate highway.
- In the *Anticipatory Anxiety* phase, your physical tension grows as you tell yourself:
  1) how frightening your symptoms may become, and
  2) how you might fail to cope during an event.
Driving toward the highway, you think, "My throat could start to close up like it did last week. That would be

7

terrifying. I'd have to pull off the road. Maybe I wouldn't even be able to breathe." In response to those thoughts, you notice yourself becoming more anxious. This process is a self-fulfilling prophecy. It is what we mean by anticipatory anxiety.

- In the *Escape* phase, your fear becomes so strong that you choose to leave the scene in order to remain in control. As you get to the exit ramp, your heart starts racing, your throat feels tight and you think, "Getting on the road now is a terrible idea!" You avoid the highway and return home instead.
- In the *Catastrophic Prediction* phase, after escaping to safety, you tell yourself just how terrible the consequences could have been if you had stayed. In this example, you say, "Thank goodness I didn't get on the road. I could have blacked out and had a wreck!"

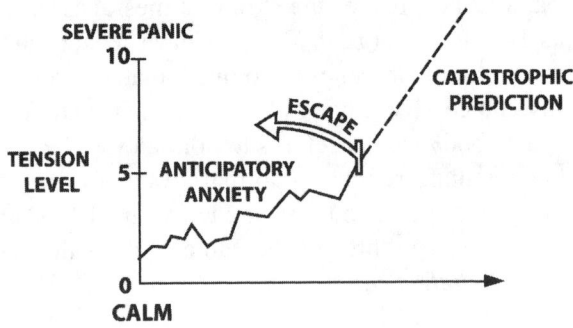

Graph 2: How fearful escape reinforces panic

So you worry before an event, leave before "the worst" happens, feel relief after you leave, and then predict how bad it would have been if you stayed. That process reinforces your fear of panic. One of the crucial lessons you will learn in this book is how to change that sequence of events.

There is a final stage of the panic cycle, *Self-doubt and Self-criticism*, that works outside the event itself, and helps attach the cyclical qualities to this condition. After struggling against the symptoms of a panic attack, people become discouraged and demoralized. They question their ability to cope. "What's wrong with me? Why do I become so afraid?" They may reinforce these doubts if their physician finds no physical cause for their frightening experiences. "It's foolish for me to have these fears, but I can't stop them. Nobody else goes through this. I'll never get better. I'll never be the same again." This final stage of the panic cycle actually supports your anticipatory anxiety, the first stage of the cycle, by repeating the pattern again.

Your Two Challenges: Conditioning and Catastrophic Predictions
Here are two important concepts that I will talk about several times as we develop strategies and activities to help break the cycle. Your panic reaction reflects a combination of unconscious *conditioning* with your conscious *predictions* of what will happen.

Conditioning is the body and mind's learning process. It is done without your awareness. Conditioning teaches you to have a fear reaction (a panic attack) to certain body sensations (like a skipped heart beat) or to particular environments (like a crowded elevator). Because this happens without you consciously noticing, you think that the anxiety attack appears from out-of-the-blue.

Predictions are your conscious interpretations of events or information and how their consequences will play out in the future. *Catastrophic Predictions* are your beliefs that something terrible will happen because of your panic symptoms. Once you have had several of these "spontaneous" panic attacks you begin consciously to scare yourself by considering three specifically detailed predictions.

- You overestimate the likelihood of having a panic attack. ("I'm sure I'll panic there.")

- You overrate how bad that panic will be. ("It will be horrible!")
- You underestimate your abilities to cope with the situation. ("I'll be overwhelmed.")

Invoking these types of predictions, combined with conditioning of your body and mind, increases the likelihood that you will panic.

To break the panic cycle, there are two big challenges you must to deal with: to manage your unconscious conditioned responses as well as your conscious exaggerated predictions. In this book, we will direct all our efforts toward changing the patterns that you have established regarding these two processes. You will learn specific ways to undo that conditioning, by repeatedly practicing exercises. You will also learn to change your predictions to others that support your ability to live without unnecessary fear.

Here is an example of how your conditioning and predictions join forces to continue the cycle of your panic attacks. Consider that a woman—I'll name her Donna—has experienced several panic attacks in grocery stores over the past two years. Today she decides to attempt the family shopping. Let's look at four parts of her experience in detail: her anticipatory anxiety, her need to escape, her catastrophic prediction after she leaves, and then her self-doubt and self-criticism.

Anticipatory Anxiety. As Donna sits at home considering the idea, she remembers her last panic attack. Soon, she begins to feel a little nervous and hesitant about today's venture. That is her unconscious, conditioned response. It comes automatically at the thought of shopping. It is also the start of her anticipatory anxiety.

Donna compounds her unconscious, generalized fear response by adding some specific worries. These worries stem from four questions she asks of herself: "How likely is something going to happen? How soon? How bad will it be? Can I cope?" In her mind, Donna has lots of thoughts and questions. But they all boil down to the responses she gives in the form of these messages: "There's a good chance I'm going to get anxious. It could happen soon. It could be a panic attack, and that would be horrible. I won't be able to cope." Now, of course, she feels even more anxiety.

She decides to do the best she can despite her fear. As Donna pulls up to the store, she hesitates again, telling herself what it might be like if she "lost control." Her anxiety level now increases for two reasons. First, she is predicting failure again. Second, her body and mind are conditioned to feel threatened at the sight of the grocery store.

As she enters the store, Donna feels a little relief when she begins to push the grocery cart, so her tension level drops slightly. While filling her cart, however, she reminds herself how long it might take to go through checkout, how she hates to be stuck in such lines. And, of course, she now notices her growing sense of physical tension. As she rounds the front end of an aisle, she sees that each checkout line has several people waiting and again tells herself that this is a threatening situation. Donna's body and mind have learned, through conditioning, to associate the longer line with threat. Now, she becomes aware of her heart. "My heart is beginning to race. I can feel the pounding. Is this the beginning of a panic attack?" As Donna is predicting an awful consequence, her level of anxiety increases still more.

Escape. As she pushes her cart down the next aisle, the tension mounts. Donna becomes more and more attentive to her body, hardly aware of the surroundings. She notices that she is feeling dizzy and immediately tells herself, "This is too much. I can't handle it. I've got to get out of here before I faint!" She leaves her cart and briskly walks from the store to the safety of her car. She has chosen escape as the only option to control the impending panic attack.

Why did Donna leave? Look at her answers to the four questions: How likely is trouble? *Very.* How soon? *Now.* How bad? *Terrible.* Can I cope? *No!* Anyone would escape the scene if those were their conclusions!

Catastrophic Prediction. As the minutes pass, Donna begins to feel normal again. She is safely outside the store now. But she revisits the episode in her mind, thinking about the worst possible outcome if she had remained in the store. "The way I was feeling, I certainly would have fainted and made a fool of myself." This catastrophic prediction—of what might have happened if she stayed—further confirms her decision to leave. At the same time, Donna's body and mind are engaged in a bout of unconscious learning that associates leaving the scene with the relief of her anxiety. So consciously and unconsciously, Donna reinforces the benefits of escape.

Self-Doubt and Self-Criticism. Imagine that for weeks after the event Donna criticizes herself. "I'll never get any better. What's wrong with me anyway? I'm too weak a person to handle these fears." If she spends ample time convincing herself of her lack of control, the next time that Donna anticipates a stressful situation what is she likely to do? She will remind herself of how she "can't cope." By telling herself how incapable she is of mastering the problem, Donna will naturally become anxious when facing her next attempt to buy the groceries.

With this example, you can see how your fearful thoughts can increase the physical sensations of anxiety. If you worry about these uncomfortable symptoms, predict that they will continue to increase given the circumstances, and predict that you are helpless to stop them, then you frighten yourself further. Every time you leave the scene in order to prevent or control a panic attack, you further convince yourself that escape is your only option. At the same time, your unconscious mind reinforces threatening associations with certain situations (being trapped) and relief with others (escaping). The good news is that we know how to correct both of those patterns. You can change your thoughts about panic once you learn that you can manage symptoms in a new way. I will be teaching you how in the remaining steps. You can also change your unconscious conditioned responses through repeated conscious actions. You will practice a whole set of exercises for that, too.

Agoraphobia and the Avoidance Cycle

If people experience a number of panic attacks over time without learning any ways to control their responses, then a new kind of cycle will evolve, the *avoidance cycle* (see Graph 3). The cycle begins in the same way, with anticipatory anxiety. The person has convinced himself that he cannot successfully cope with his feared symptoms or the event, and that if he tries to overcome his anxiety he will fail. To avoid having a panic attack, he decides to stay away from any threatening situation. Thus, avoidance becomes the second phase. And, the more he avoids, the more he continues to feel doubt and settle into a state of self-criticism, which is the third phase. With doubt and self-criticism, he feels less certain about his ability to face a fearful situation in the future, which reinforces his anticipatory anxiety and sets the avoidance cycle into motion again. When a person with panic disorder starts avoiding a number of significant events, the condition is called agoraphobia. We can also call this avoidance cycle the *agoraphobia cycle*. The effect of the avoidance cycle is that the person feels safer, but his world becomes much smaller.

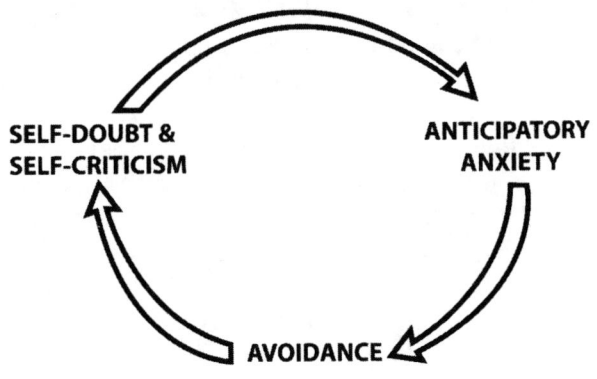

Graph 3: The avoidance of cycle (Agoraphobia Cycle)

Breaking Free of the Panic Cycle
Now that you have seen how the cycle of panic works, it is time to learn how to break free of it. Adopting a number of self-help skills will help you regain control of your life. You should know that these skills are not magic, they can't make the causes of your anxiety disappear. Stresses and tension are a normal part of adult living. No skills, regardless of their power, can remove the ordinary concerns of responsible adults to the give and take of everyday life. However, no one's life needs to be controlled by panic attacks. With the support of a loving community, with the advice of caring professionals, and with your own dedicated persistence, you can break free of this seemingly perpetual cycle of panic and return to a positive, active life.

This book can be one of your resources, offering you a combination of knowledge and skills. To prepare you for the skills and exercises that will help you conquer the panic cycle, you must learn about some of the body's processes and behaviors that are connected with the symptoms of anxiety. **Step 2** of our self-help sequences focuses on how your body purposely creates both tension and relaxation. You will be able to use this information as you begin practicing skills in **Step 3**.

STEP 2: Learn about Conditioning and the Body's Special Emergency Response

Let's look more closely at how the body and mind unconsciously respond to threat. What are the stages of this response and how does it become "conditioned," meaning: how does it start happening automatically, without your awareness?

Most people who have panic attacks describe the experience as feeling instantly out-of-control. They emphasize losing control of their body. All of a sudden, physical symptoms come rushing into their awareness and they feel overwhelmed.

Although panic does seem to occur instantaneously, there are a number of activities that take place in a silent communication from our mind to our body in the highly compressed span of time leading up to that moment. If we could magically slow down this process, we would find that a person's anticipatory anxiety involves several unconscious messages communicated in a matter of seconds. That is why panic can feel like such a surprise: we cannot *consciously* be aware of the mind's *unconscious* messages prior to a panic attack.

Yet these unconscious messages instruct the body to change in ways that make you anxious. In this step, you will learn how it happens. Later, you will learn how to fix the things that go wrong and result in panic attack.

Here is the central point of this step. Our genes carry information, a set of instructions, which has developed over thousands of generations of learning and conditioning, to protect us from threat. When you have a panic attack, your body is performing wonderfully! It is doing exactly what it is supposed to do: respond to an emergency. How does it know there is an emergency? Your body is designed to trust the mind's assessment of the situation. Our goal is *not* to fix how your body is reacting, because it is not broken. Your reactions are a finely honed response that answers with a moment's notice to the warning, "This is an emergency." It responds the same way *every* *time* to *any* event that the mind calls an emergency.

Instead of trying to fix the body, we will focus on changing the communication from your mind to your body. We will change your faulty conscious messages and unconscious messages, those that tell your body to go into emergency mode when, actually, there is no emergency.

How can we do this? When we become mentally involved with a past event, our mind tends to tell our body to respond to that experience as though the event were happening *right now*. All of us have this experience. For instance, you might flip through the pages of your wedding album and begin to feel some of the same excitement and joy you felt on your wedding day. That is your unconscious mind pulling up memories of your pleasure. Those memories include a very simple instruction given to your body: respond as though that day were right now. Perhaps on another day someone mentions the death of a close friend. You, in turn, unconsciously recall the death of someone you love, and you begin to feel sad. The mind's simple message to the body? "Act as though that day is now. Generate sadness."

Here is how this process occurs during panic, illustrated in Graph 4, on page 18. As you consider approaching a situation where you have panicked in the past, your conditioning begins to influence your reactions. Through association, your unconscious mind spontaneously retrieves a blueprint of a previous panic episode. It instantly tells your body to "respond as though the past is happening right now." And you suddenly are conscious of being scared. Your conscious mind isn't aware of this silent communication. You are more likely to interpret what happened like this: "I simply had the thought of going into a restaurant, and I was suddenly anxious."

So, first you contemplate facing a feared situation, and that unconsciously reminds you of your past failures. Since you are now anxious just *thinking* about the event, you next begin to question your coping abilities. "Can I really handle this? What if I panic again?" Your unconscious mind silently responds to these rhetorical questions by creating more sensations of anxiety, which you interpret as warning-sign answers to your own thoughts: "No, based on my past performances I don't think I can handle it. If I panic I will totally lose control." These unconscious statements present this basic instruction to your body: "Guard against the worst possible outcome, as though it's about to happen!" Your body responds impeccably. It produces a complex set of physical changes to protect you from danger.

Notice that your unconscious mind doesn't keep memories tucked away securely in the past. You might be thinking about an incident of six months ago, but your mind treats it as a current event. The more realistically your unconscious mind considers entering that situation, the more your mind says to your body, "The danger is NOW. Guard me! Protect me!" This is how anticipatory anxiety turns into a panic attack.

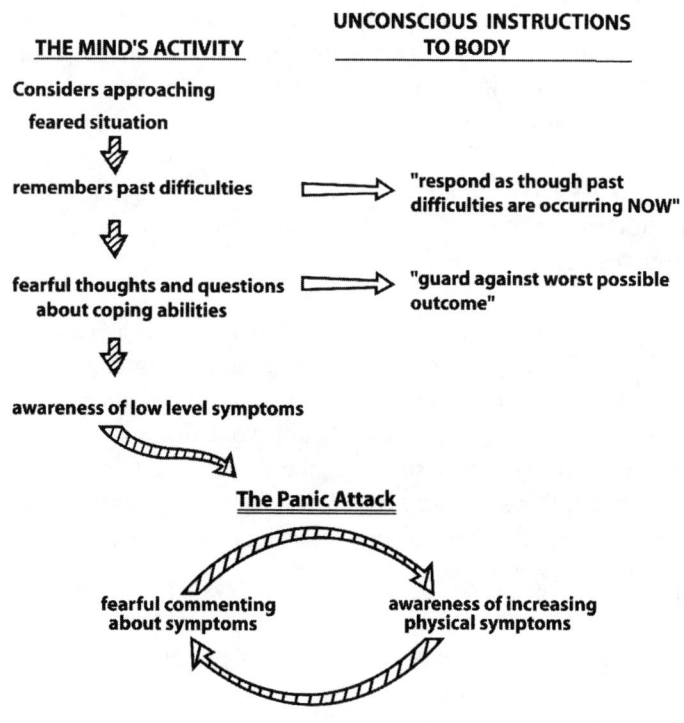

Graph 4: The first two stages of the panic cycle

In a panic attack, these messages are no longer just silent. You notice those physical sensations that the body undergoes, such as an increasingly rapid heartbeat. Then you become afraid of them and begin to make fearful comments about the symptoms ("Oh, no! I'm feeling even worse!") In this way, you unconsciously instruct your body to protect you. It begins a change in chemistry in order to guard against the existing emergency. Yet, since this is not a true physical crisis, you can't properly use the body's power effectively. But, since its preparedness continues to develop, you notice an increase in physical symptoms. This creates a closed-loop, reinforcing cycle during the panic attack, as shown at the bottom of Graph 4. You notice your symptoms, you become afraid of them, your fear tells your body to create more physical changes, and that frightens you even more.

Let's look a little more closely at this physiology, which is often misunderstood during panic. Table 3, on page 20, lists many of the physical changes that take place when we flip on that emergency switch. Technically, we are stimulating hormones that engage the sympathetic branch of the autonomic nervous system. All those changes prepare the body to respond to an actual crisis. For instance, the eyes dilate to improve vision, the heart rate increases to circulate blood more quickly to vital organs, respiration increases to provide more oxygen to the rapidly circulating blood, the muscles tense in the arms and legs in order to move quickly and precisely.

These are normal, healthy, lifesaving changes in the body's physiology. When there is an actual emergency, we hardly notice these changes; we pay attention to the crisis, instead. When we are reacting to a "pseudo-emergency" of panic and not a real threat, two problems develop. First, we are stuck focusing on our fearful thoughts and our physical sensations instead of taking action to solve the problem. Because of this, we are not expressing our body's energy directly by physical activity, and our tension and anxiety continue to build.

TABLE 3: THE BODY'S EMERGENCY RESPONSE (SYMPATHETIC RESPONSE)

- blood sugar level increases
- eyes dilate
- sweat glands perspire
- heart rate increases
- mouth becomes dry
- muscles tense
- blood decreases in arms and legs and pools in head and trunk

The second problem has to do with breathing. During an emergency, both breathing rate and pattern change. Instead of breathing slowly and gently from our lower lungs, we begin to breathe rapidly and shallowly from our upper lungs. This shift not only increases the amount of oxygen flowing into our bloodstream, it also quickly "blows off" an increasing amount of carbon dioxide. In a physical emergency, we produce excess carbon dioxide through our physical response to the danger, so this breathing pattern is essential. When we are not physically exerting ourselves to manage the crisis, the change in breathing produces the phenomenon called *hyperventilation*, by discharging too much carbon dioxide.

Understanding hyperventilation is crucial to your goal of breaking the panic cycle. During the anticipatory anxiety and the panic attack stages of the cycle, hyperventilation can produce most of the uncomfortable sensations that we notice. These are broken down in Table 4. If we can simply find a way to change how we breathe during panic-provoking times, we ought to be able to significantly reduce these uncomfortable symptoms. You will learn how in the next step.

TABLE 4: POSSIBLE SYMPTOMS DURING HYPERVENTILATION

- irregular heart rate
- dizziness, lightheadedness
- shortness of breath
- "asthma"
- choking sensations
- lump in throat
- difficulty swallowing
- heartburn
- chest pain
- blurred vision
- numbness or tingling of mouth, hands, feet
- muscle pains or spasms
- shaking
- nausea
- fatigue, weakness
- confusion, inability to concentrate

Summary

Before you can learn to gain control over panic, you must first believe that you have the ability to take control. You may feel helplessly out-of-control, experiencing panic as something that rushes over you from out-of-the-blue. Panic attacks have a real, identifiable origin. They develop from a coupling of your conscious interpretations and predictions of an event or situation with your own unconscious responses to it, which are caused by conditioning. A successful self-help program addresses those conscious thoughts as well as your conditioning. It also directs you to increase your activities in the world, because experience will be your greatest teacher.

As you continue reading this book, here are some important ideas to keep in mind:
1. Our body responds to the messages it receives from the mind. If we label a situation as dangerous, and then begin to approach that situation, the body will secrete hormones to prepare physically for the crisis. Even if the situation is relatively safe, if the mind *interprets* it as unsafe, the body responds to that message of "danger."
2. Many of your reactions to fearful situations are conditioned responses, happening unconsciously and automatically. That's why you suddenly get scared in places that are actually safe.
3. Within the panic cycle, your body is responding appropriately. It is *not* the problem.
4. When your mind tells your body to protect you from danger, your body produces a good, strong, healthy physical response. The sensations you feel from this response may frighten you, because they are designed to happen quickly and powerfully. This is how you want your body to respond in an emergency. You never know when you need to avoid a deer in the road, or catch someone who is slipping on the icy sidewalk.
5. You can unlearn this conditioned response and learn to respond in a new way. You will learn how in the remaining steps.
6. When any of us become anxious, our rate and pattern of breathing changes. These changes can produce hyperventilation, which may cause many of the uncomfortable physical symptoms during panic. Sometimes, changing the way we breathe will reduce uncomfortable symptoms. You will learn how to do that in the next step.

STEP 3: Practice the Calming Skills

In Step 2, you learned that your breathing pattern as well as your thoughts directly affect your body's chemistry to produce physical symptoms through the nervous system's emergency response – the sympathetic response of the autonomic nervous system. In this step, you will learn how to alter those sensations, how to bring your body back in balance through proper breathing and muscle relaxation. By shifting your breathing rate and pattern, and by helping your muscles relax, you can stimulate the nervous system's counter response – the body's equally powerful and functionally opposite parasympathetic system. We often call this the relaxation response. For our purposes, we will call it the *calming response*.

Table 5, on page 24, lists the physical changes that take place during the calming response. As you can see, this process reverses all of the primary changes of the emergency response. Your heart slows down, muscles relax and you feel calm. But these two physical processes are not exactly like mirror images of one another. One of the important differences between them involves time. The emergency response takes place instantly in what we call "mass action." All the changes occur together. In the calming response they do not. Once we flip that emergency switch on, it takes a while to turn it off and shut the process down by rebalancing the chemistry. In other words, the body needs time to respond to our calming skills. For this reason, it is important for you to know what specific skills will reverse the emergency response to help calm your body and clear your mind. And, you have to develop trust that they will work, since they aren't supposed to work instantly.

TABLE 5: THE CALMING RESPONSE (PARASYMPATHETIC RESPONSE)

- oxygen consumption decreases
- breathing slows
- heart rate slows
- blood pressure decreases
- muscle tension decreases
- growing sense of ease in body, calmness in mind

Here are two breathing skills and one formal technique you can use to produce the calming response. In later steps, you will learn how to change your fearful thinking, because each time you frighten yourself with catastrophic thoughts you also re-stimulate your body's emergency response. To begin with, however, you need a solid foundation in proper breathing and muscle relaxation.

Calming Your Breath
The first breathing skill is called "Natural Breathing." We all should use this breathing pattern whenever we are not involved in physical activity. Consider practicing this breathing frequently through the day, since it provides for sufficient oxygen intake and controls the exhalation of carbon dioxide.

NATURAL BREATHING

1. Gently and slowly inhale a normal amount of air through your nose, filling only your lower lungs (your stomach will expand while your upper chest remains still).

2. Exhale easily.

3. Continue this gentle breathing pattern with a relaxed attitude, concentrating on filling only the lower lungs.

This breathing pattern is different from the breathing pattern that automatically takes over during anxious moments. Instead of breathing rapidly and shallowly into the upper lungs, which expands the chest, you breathe gently into the lower lungs, expanding the abdomen.

The second technique is deep diaphragmatic breathing. You can use it when you are feeling anxious or panicky because it is a powerful way to control hyperventilation, slow a rapid heartbeat and promote physical comfort. For this reason, it is called the "Calming Breath."

CALMING BREATH

1. Take a long, slow inhale, first filling your lower lungs (you will see your belly protrude), then your upper lungs.

2. Hold your breath to the count of "three."

3. Exhale slowly, while you relax the muscles in your face, jaw, shoulders, and stomach.

Practice this Calming Breath at least ten times a day for several weeks. Use it during times of transition, between projects or whenever you want to let go of tension and begin to experience a sense of calmness. Then, when you need a tool to help you calm down during panic, you will be more familiar and comfortable with the process.

Quieting Your Body

If you are experiencing panic attacks, you can benefit from a self-help approach that enables you to control the early signs of tension so that your anxiety level does not grow to panic proportions. Natural Breathing and Calming Breath can help.

Now, let's broaden our efforts. Here is another simple, straightforward method to reduce your stress and anxiety. This technique is a shortened version of Dr. Edmond Jacobson's "progressive relaxation," which is one of the most widely researched and respected forms of muscle relaxation in the health field. Physicians and psychologists have used it for more than 60 years.

We know that each time you have a fearful thought your body responds by becoming a little tense. What if you ignore that physical tension and focus instead on your fearful thoughts (which bring more tension)? Eventually, your body's physical response will grow to a level of tension that forces you to take notice. By that point, these sensations might feel as though they are too strong to control.

Why would practicing a muscle relaxation technique be useful here? There are the four primary psychological benefits of this technique:
1. You will learn to be more aware of any low levels of muscle tension during your day. It is much easier to control tension when you are able to respond to its early signs.
2. You will learn how to relax systematically the major muscles of your body on a daily basis. This reduces the chance of small tensions piling up day after day.
3. With practice, over time your body learns how to release tensions more quickly based on your own suggestions.
4. You will be preparing your body to learn to briefly let go of tensions when the panic cycle begins.

There are a variety of ways in which the mind can learn something new. One powerful way is through a dramatic experience. Another is through repetition. A panic attack is a dramatic (traumatic) event that becomes etched in memory. After a panic attack, we tend to call up that frightening memory easily as we consider entering a similar situation, and we suddenly feel anxious. This is the conditioning process we have been discussing.

Muscle relaxation techniques are one way to counteract that traumatic memory, and we learn those skills through repetition instead of drama. Only through repetitive practice can you expect to develop a powerful enough opposing force to the tensions and anxiety of panic. It is important that you commit time on a daily basis to build the skill of muscle relaxation.

The following five-minute exercise is one of many you can use.

The Technique. To practice this skill, find a quiet room where you will not be disturbed for a few minutes. Sit in a comfortable chair and loosen any tight clothing. Close your eyes and take three deep, slow diaphragmatic breaths (Calming Breaths). Begin an easy, gentle breathing pattern, preferably breathing into your abdomen instead of into your upper chest (Natural Breathing). Sit quietly for two minutes, letting go of any distracting thoughts. Just let your mind drift easily, pleasantly.

Then, one by one, tighten and relax the four groups of muscles described here. Squeeze those muscles tightly for about ten seconds, and then relax them for 15 – 20 seconds. Here are the groups:

GROUP 1: ARMS, SHOULDERS, CHEST AND NECK.
Bend your arms, and then cross them in front of your chest. (Your elbows will be pointing down, your fists pointing up.) Tighten your fists, arms, shoulders, chest and neck while you continue to breathe gently. Hold these muscles tense for ten seconds. Now, let go and allow these muscles to relax for 15 – 20 seconds.

GROUP 2: FACE. Squeeze the muscles of your face together, as though you've just bitten into a lemon. Purse your lips, and bite down on your teeth to tense your jaw. Hold this position for ten seconds as you continue to breathe gently. Now, let go and allow these muscles to relax for 15 – 20 seconds.

GROUP 3: STOMACH AND LOWER BACK. Take a deep breath and pull in your stomach as far as you can. Tense the muscles in your lower back. Hold your breath as you silently count to "six" in this position. Now, *slowly* exhale and let these muscles relax for 15 – 20 seconds.

GROUP 4: LEGS. Extend your legs straight out, propping them on a footstool if you want. Tense all your leg muscles as you point your toes toward your head. Hold this position for ten seconds as you continue to breathe gently. Now, let go and allow these muscles to relax for 15 – 20 seconds.

Go through these four muscle group exercises a second time before continuing.

Now, let your entire body become limp and loose, and your mind quiet, as you visualize yourself in some pleasant, relaxing scene, such as lying on the beach, floating on a cloud, or enjoying a stroll in a peaceful environment. Let your body enjoy a good feeling of warmth and heaviness. Remain focused on this scene for one or two minutes, then slowly open your eyes.

DAILY MUSCLE RELAXATION

1. Find a private place and a comfortable chair, close your eyes and sit quietly, letting go of any distracting thoughts. (2 minutes)
2. Tense your arms, shoulders, chest and neck.
   (10 seconds) Now relax. (15 – 20 seconds)
3. Tense your face. (10 seconds) Now relax. (15-20 seconds)
4. Take a deep breath. Pull in your stomach and tense your lower back. Hold your breath while counting to "six." Then exhale *slowly*. Now relax. (15-20 seconds)
5. Extend your legs and tense them. (10 seconds) Now relax. (15-20 seconds)
6. Repeat Steps 2-5.
7. Visualize a pleasant scene as you invite your body to feel relaxed, warm and heavy. (2 minutes)
8. Open your eyes, feeling refreshed and at ease.

Practice this ten-minute technique daily, once in the morning and once in the evening. And use it any other time you would like to feel more physically comfortable.

Tracking Your Practice

Use the chart below to help remind you to practice these breathing skills and muscle exercises every day. Place a check mark each morning and evening that you practice the Deep Muscle Relaxation technique. In the daily box below Natural Breathing, place a check mark each time you pause during the day to practice breathing gently into your lower lungs. Your goal is ten check marks per day. In the Calming Breath box, place a check mark each time you practice taking a Calming Breath, and try for ten practices a day. This is a one-week schedule. You can make a copy of the form to track several weeks. Set a goal of five weeks of daily practice, using Chart 1.

Day	Deep Muscle Relaxation* AM PM		Natural Breathing* (goal: 10/day)	Calming Breath* (goal: 10/day)
Chart 1: Practicing the Calming Skills				
Monday				
Tuesday				
Wednesday				
Thursday				
Friday				
Saturday				
Sunday				

* Place √ for each practice.
Print out a full size version of this chart from the ADAA website at www.adaa.org.

A Special Note

In the next three steps, I suggest that you practice a number of exercises without using any special breathing skills to help you relax. I will label "practicing a breathing skill" or "trying to relax" as *safety crutches*. This may seem to contradict my suggestions in this step, so let me explain.

I am encouraging you to develop two approaches which work together to help you get stronger. First, in this step, I want you to learn how to calm your body and quiet your thoughts. This teaches you that your body really does know how to let go of tension. You will be able to use these skills whenever you want to calm down. You can also use them before and after any of the exercises in the coming steps.

In the second approach, you will challenge your belief that you *must* relax to control your panic attacks, or to prevent some catastrophe caused by your panic. You may think that taking a calming breath will prevent you from having a heart attack during panic, or that calming yourself down will stop you from going crazy during panic. These catastrophic fears can keep you from fully recovering from panic attacks. Steps 4, 5 and 6 will help you learn that you can master panic best by confronting each of these fears directly.

It is fine to use relaxation and breathing skills to help calm yourself down. In the coming steps, your practice will not include focusing on relaxation during the exercises. Once you have mastered the skills of Steps 4, 5 and 6, then you will have the option of using either approach. Step 7 discusses your choices.

STEP 4: Adopt a New Self-Help Strategy

A panic attack is nothing more than an extension of a normal fear response. It is *not* an indication that something is dramatically wrong with your body, only that your body is responding strongly to certain cues.

Panic attacks can lead to panic disorder when three things occur:
1. Your body and mind become conditioned (unconsciously trained) to get anxious when you notice uncomfortable symptoms or when you approach the situations where you have panicked in the past.
2. You continue to frighten yourself by worrying about your past panics and your potential upcoming panics.
3. You avoid those situations, or you adopt special behaviors to help you avoid symptoms in those situations.

To break the cycle of panic, you need to deal with each of these parts of the problem. Coming up in Steps 5 and 6, you will practice skills that will help in that process. Here is a summary of what you will achieve:
1. You will learn to generate, voluntarily and purposely, your fearful symptoms. During that time, you will discover that the symptoms occur naturally and are uncomfortable but not dangerous.
2. You will study all the ways you try to keep the symptoms from getting worse – what I call your "safety crutches" – and you will stop doing them. Again, you will learn that the symptoms are uncomfortable but not overwhelming.
3. You will repeatedly practice voluntarily creating your symptoms in a variety of locations, including your most feared situations. This will condition (unconsciously train) your body and mind to respond to those situations with less anxiety.

These suggestions may seem threatening: you must commit voluntarily and purposely to being scared and uncomfortable for a while. Putting that decision into practice will be quite hard. It will require that, during specific times of the day, you will not focus on calming down through breathing skills and relaxation. During other times of your day, relaxing and calming down will be quite useful and appropriate. To master certain skills, you will need to let yourself feel distress again and again for brief periods. The good news is that this approach represents the most up-to-date recommendations of the best panic researchers and clinicians in the world today. Researchers have studied this type of process and have proven that it works for many people. This strategy is helping thousands of panic attack sufferers recover from their fear and avoidance. And it can help you break your panic cycle.

The next set of procedures will help you reach your goal of ending panic's control over your life. You must bring courage, time, concentration and effort to the task. Together we will get the job done. When you succeed, feel free to send me an email (rrw@med.unc.edu) about how you did it. If you follow these instructions for several weeks and are making no progress, then write me to explain how you are having trouble and I will help you if I can. If you need additional help along the way, there are suggestions in the back of this book on locating a mental health professional – a counselor, social worker, therapist, psychologist or psychiatrist – who is a member of the Anxiety Disorders Association of America, and who specializes in anxiety disorders. This person can assist you in your self-help efforts.

In order to win back control of your life, you will have to challenge some of your most basic assumptions. You have made decisions in the past about how you will respond to anxiety and panic. As we have seen, some of those decisions are having the opposite effect. They are actually *promoting* the symptoms you are trying to get rid of. The biggest decision you have made is to consciously attempt to keep panic under control, to keep the symptoms from becoming stronger. However, that is the most important decision you must change. This may seem hard to believe and even quite illogical. I am sure it will seem even harder to *do*. You must reverse that decision – of controlling symptoms, keeping them in check, not letting them get stronger – if you are going to win over panic.

Here is the basic strategy. **Get anxious on purpose. Once you are anxious, *encourage* the symptoms to continue for a long time. During this time, stop worrying and start supporting yourself. Let go of your safety crutches. Do this over and over, in all your fearful situations.**

In the coming steps, you will see how you can put these principles into action. First, let's look at each of the specific points of your new strategy.

Get anxious on purpose.
Your old strategy was to try not to get anxious. You wanted to stay as calm and relaxed as possible when you approached a threatening situation. This is *not* how you get over panic attacks. Instead, you need to practice skills that help you on two fronts. The first deals with your conscious beliefs about all the terrible consequences that stem from a panic attack. The other focuses on helping your unconscious mind "unlearn" the panic response.

The first way this approach will help is by having you confront your faulty beliefs. It makes sense that you have been trying to avoid anxiety, because you feared your bodily sensations and their consequences. Becoming anxious often led to having an anxiety attack. You also feared that a panic attack would lead to something even worse: you would cause a scene, not be able to breathe, or become trapped and not be able to get back home. These are what we referred to

33

in Step 1 as *catastrophic predictions*, the terrible events you imagine will occur if you don't stay in control.

The point of facing your symptoms directly is not simply to become anxious. By using this approach, you can learn that the catastrophic predictions you associate with those sensations do not occur. You don't go crazy, faint, have a heart attack or humiliate yourself. Please keep this in mind as you study these next steps: *the essence of recovering from panic attacks is to confront directly your worst fantasies of what might happen if you panic.*

The second way this approach will help is by giving your mind time to "unlearn" the panic response discussed in Step 2. You need to get your conscious mind – including all your worries about something bad happening – out of the way so that your unconscious mind and your body can learn their skills. Instead of consciously trying to avoid anxiety, you need to look for *opportunities* to get anxious. Instead of trying to get rid of your symptoms, you need purposely to *generate* them. Instead of avoiding fearful situations, you need to go *toward* them. Your goal is to create opportunities to become anxious and panicky, and then voluntarily encourage those feelings.

This step is so important to your recovery. That is why – in the exercises of Steps 5 and 6 – you are encouraged *not* to practice the breathing and relaxation skills from Step 3. Those calming skills will be helpful in the future, and you should practice them by using Chart 1. However, your mind also needs time to face the anxiety directly, without trying to fight it or trying to relax. Once you reach Step 7 ("Now, Greet Panic in Your Daily Life"), you have the choice to use those breathing skills during anxious times.

By trying to get anxious on purpose, you will train your mind to react more sensibly to events, instead of over-reacting with panic. This will not occur after one or two events. You will need to face those uncomfortable feelings many times in order to develop your competence. It will take repetition and concentration. It will happen. You will succeed.

When you are about to practice facing a fearful situation, you are likely to be scared. Expect that. In fact, being scared should be one of your cues that you are practicing the right task. Going forward while you feel frightened is the definition of courage. Don't turn back in the face of your discomfort.

When you face the situations you have been avoiding, you will occasionally trigger a panic attack. That sounds quite intimidating, but experiencing the emotions and physical sensations of panic is fundamental to the success of your work. Unless you learn that you can survive panic, you will always fear and avoid panic. True, you have had plenty of panic attacks in the past, and that hasn't gotten you better! *Having* the panic attack is not the key. How you are consciously *responding* to it is what counts. Instead of gritting your teeth and bearing up the best you can, you will be dropping your guard and trying to make the symptoms stronger. I bet you haven't done much of that yet! When you do, then the more panic attacks you have, the more confidence you will gain, and the faster your brain and body can learn that the sensations aren't harmful.

The best way to reduce the symptoms of panic is to stop wanting to reduce them! Practice generating your symptoms in order to accept your symptoms. Don't escape. Willingly stay with your feelings.

Once you are anxious, encourage the symptoms to continue for a long time.
In your old strategy, you wanted to get rid of your symptoms as soon as you noticed them. In fact, clinicians have long encouraged people to master special breathing techniques and relaxation methods, similar to those in Step 3. This seemed to imply that you should calm down when facing your fears.

We now believe, however, that it is better if you also have practice sessions where you are directly facing your anxiety while not applying those relaxation skills. During these times, when you are practicing your skills, your goal will be to *want* to get as anxious as you can. This is a great way to defeat panic. Don't seek to get rid of your symptoms, seek to have more of them! Why? Over time, as you consciously encourage your symptoms, your body and mind unconsciously learn to end the panic attacks. The next two steps will explain how to practice this.

Not only should you encourage your symptoms, you should try to stay uncomfortable for a long time. When anxiety hits, your instincts tell you to fight it or get away from it. It's the American way: "Don't just stand there, do something!" Take the opposite stance: stand there and wait it out. Don't act on your impulse to run. Your body and mind need prolonged time, again and again, to unlearn the panic reaction. We often recommend that each practice session last for 45-90 minutes. Brief contact with your symptoms is far less effective than longer exposure.

Anxiety wins over people who are intimidated by it and try to hide from it. To keep from being blackmailed by your panicky symptoms, step out in the open and look for ways to bring on your symptoms. Don't run from your symptoms, run *toward* them. Your body will learn best within the arena of voluntary discomfort.

Find as many situations as you can, as often as you can, to practice your skills. Frequent practice is the key to success. Ask yourself, "What can I do to get myself uncomfortable today?" (Again, I'm sure you notice how silly that suggestion sounds. That's how you know it is the right idea. All the important changes you need to make will seem paradoxical, which means the opposite of logic). Accepting and tolerating your physical symptoms is important. Don't stop there. Try to *increase* them. In this approach, you encourage all uncomfortable physical symptoms to get *stronger.* Tell your heart to beat faster! Ask you legs to turn to jelly! Instruct your hands to shake even more! Encourage your head to get dizzier! Frightening as this may sound, it is one of the most direct ways to win over panic.

During this time, stop worrying and start supporting yourself.

Notice that the strategy so far is to *encourage* your feelings (being scared) and your physical sensations (heart racing, dizziness, and so forth). At the same time, you need to *discourage* your worried thoughts. This second big task is just as essential as the first.

There is a simple equation your mind might use in order to determine how worried it should be about an upcoming event:

$$\text{Worry} = \frac{\text{How likely is it to happen?} + \text{How soon will it happen?} + \text{How bad will it be?}}{\text{How will I cope with it?}}$$

To worry, you must factor together your judgments about the likelihood of the event occurring, how soon it will happen and how bad it will be. Those three viewpoints are related to, or, in the case of our equation, divided by, the degree to which you think you can cope with whatever takes place. Remember the example of Donna, in Step 1? I described how her negative predictions about going to the grocery increased her anxiety and fear. Based on your past experience, you have probably answered these questions the way Donna did. As you approach a situation where you have panicked in the past, or if you begin to feel sensations that you associate with an impending panic attack, here is what you might say:

$$\text{Worry about panic} = \frac{\text{There is a good chance I am going to get anxious} + \text{It's starting to happen now} + \text{It could become a severe panic attack and that would be horrible!}}{\text{I can't cope with that! I'll fall apart!}}$$

37

In other words, you say, "It's highly likely, very soon, that I will feel horrible, and there is nothing I can do about it!" No wonder you avoid these situations! Who wouldn't!?

It is important that you know these worries don't just predict problems. They actually generate much of your discomfort and avoidance. Thinking about these horrible outcomes makes you even more anxious. If you get anxious enough, you will decide to steer away from those threatening situations.

Your goal is to change *worrying about panic to purposely choosing to approach panic.* You will do this, over time, by learning to change two of the four statements that your mind plugs into the equation. I will show you how in the coming steps. Now your job is to understand the concept behind the change. Here is what the change looks like:

Choose to approach panic	=	There is a good chance I am going to get anxious	+	It's starting to happen now I will handle it	+	It could be a panic attack and that will be uncomfortable

As you choose to approach panic, you will learn to change "The panic attack will be *horrible,*" to "The panic attack will be *uncomfortable.*" You will also change "I can't cope with it," to "I will handle it." These two changes work together. You will be much more likely to consider handling sensations that you believe will be uncomfortable instead of those that you predict will be horrible. Let's study all parts of this equation in its new form:

"Choose to approach panic."	→	That is the current goal we have been discussing: Instead of running from panic, you are going to go toward it.
"There is a good chance I am going to get anxious."	→	That is your intention: to get anxious on purpose.
"It's starting to happen now."	→	Good! You need to get anxious to help your unconscious mind learn that it isn't so threatening.
"It could be a panic attack, and that will be uncomfortable."	→	This is the new piece I want you to consider. When you predict it will be severe and horrible, you scare yourself too much.
"I will handle it."	→	Through the exercises in Steps 5 and 6, you will learn ways to cope with your symptoms, including panic, so they will feel uncomfortable but not horrible. Your short-term goal is to have symptoms and *manage* them. That will be how your unconscious mind learns to get rid of panic.

You must learn to stay rational in the face of intense fear and to resist your powerful urge to escape. This is no easy feat. You will get there, in part, by learning to observe your thoughts, feelings and sensations with objective detachment. Let's start with controlling your worries. When you hear yourself saying, "Oh, no, I'm starting to feel anxious! This is terrible!" you need to begin saying, "Oh, yes. I'm anxious. My heart's racing. I'm scared. This is hard but good. I need the practice. I'm just going to stay here with these feelings for a bit. I don't need to fix them. I can handle it."

You can evaluate your sensations as strong, very intense, or uncomfortable. Practice not judging them as "too much," "overwhelming," "horrible," or "terrifying."

In the feared situation, create a sense of safety. Practice giving yourself positive messages such as:
"It's OK that I'm anxious right now."
"I'll be fine no matter what I feel."
"I'm scared, and I'm safe."
"It's OK to take a chance here. This is a place to practice my skills."
"I can handle these symptoms."

These messages, and others like them, help you learn to stay in the present with your feelings and physical sensations. You don't have to *do* anything. Notice your sensations, notice your feelings, and simply stay with them for a time. This takes a great deal of courage. When you are courageous, you will be surprised what good things happen as you practice!

Let go of your safety crutches.

You might be thinking, "I have already been exposed to these anxious feelings repeatedly and I haven't gotten any better at coping with them. How is this approach any different?" Most people facing fearful situations have coping strategies that they believe keep them safe. They might think, "As long as I keep rolling the windows down and turning up the radio when I'm driving the car, I will keep myself from passing out." The underlying belief is "I will pass out if I don't do these things." Even though you continue to drive while rolling down the windows and turning up the radio, you remain nervous about the possibility of passing out. It is these false beliefs – in this case that "I will pass out" – that keep you distressed. The approach taken here will address these catastrophic fears directly.

You are familiar with the most obvious way that you avoid becoming anxious: you stay away from situations that might provoke your fear. There is another way too. Once you are in the situation, you have a variety of actions that:
- reduce any scary sensations
- make it easier for you to escape, or
- make it easier to get help if you need it

Perhaps you carry a closed container of water into the mall in case your mouth gets too dry and you feel like you can't swallow. Maybe you push a cart in the grocery store instead of carrying a basket, because it makes you feel more stable. You might press your hands onto the podium when you give a speech so that your hands stop shaking. All of these types of actions make sense if you are trying to reduce your symptoms. These "safety crutches" actually make you work harder to get better. You should identify behaviors like these and work on getting rid of them.

If you broke your leg, you would use crutches for a few weeks to assist your body in healing. Over time, however, you would need to remove those crutches to let your leg become strong again. In a similar way, safety crutches can be helpful, and I am sure you have some crutches you have used to get you through some tough times with panic. But your body and mind need to get strong if they are going to mend. Safety crutches prevent you from completing that healing process. How do safety crutches interfere with your goals?

- They buffer you from your anxiety. They put an obstacle between you and anxiety. You need to face directly your symptoms without resistance, so your body learns more quickly how to become less anxious.
- They prevent you from learning that your worst worries don't come true. You exaggerate either your predictions about how bad the symptoms will be, how negatively others will act toward you, or how poorly you will cope with the situation. When

you introduce behaviors that make you feel safe, you don't get to challenge fully those beliefs. Instead, you need to be completely clear about what actually happens when you face your fears head on.
- They persuade you that it is the safety crutches themselves that protect you from stronger symptoms, or from catastrophe ("If I hadn't held on to that wall, then I clearly would have fallen over"). This keeps you from discovering that if you had done *nothing* special, your symptoms would still not have increased, and there would still be no catastrophe.

Trying to relax in a threatening situation is certainly understandable. Taking a nice Calming Breath, as I described in Step 3, might make you feel better. But applying relaxation skills is also a safety crutch, a way you try to avoid feeling anxious. I will be suggesting exercises for you to do in later steps during which I encourage you to purposely avoid any brief relaxation skills. I will do this for the reasons I just described. Consciously, you need to know that even if you drop all your safety crutches, nothing terrible happens. Unconsciously, your mind and body need direct access to your anxiety to help unlearn the panic response.

Table 6 offers examples of safety crutches. See how many you can relate to. Place a check next to those you use in threatening situations. We will work with this list again in Steps 5 and 6.

TABLE 6: SAFETY CRUTCHES
SECURITY PROPS ☐ Carry a cell phone ☐ Carry an anti-anxiety pill in your pocket ☐ Carry water ☐ Bring things that feel, taste, smell or sound good (rabbits' feet, Koosh® balls, Silly Putty®, candy, Ipod)

- ☐ Wear lucky clothes
- ☐ Repeat prayers or lucky phrases
- ☐ Bring a friend or family member
- ☐ Carry phone numbers to call in "emergency"
- ☐ Carry a book or other distraction object

RELAXATION
- ☐ Try to stay relaxed
- ☐ Practice relaxation skills
- ☐ Practice breathing skills

MONITORING
- ☐ Monitor your thoughts
- ☐ Monitor your physical sensations
- ☐ Check your pulse
- ☐ Check your breathing
- ☐ Try to swallow
- ☐ Watch yourself carefully
- ☐ Watch others carefully
- ☐ Time your symptoms
- ☐ Watch the clock
- ☐ Check the weather
- ☐ Check the exits/pathways/route ahead

ESCAPE & ESCAPE PLANS
- ☐ Sit close to the exit or on the end of the row
- ☐ Sit in the back
- ☐ Know where the exit is
- ☐ Know where the bathroom is
- ☐ Prepare an excuse for leaving
- ☐ Know where closest hospital is

REASSURANCE
- ☐ Look for a friendly face
- ☐ Constantly reassure yourself
- ☐ Remind yourself you can leave
- ☐ Get reassurance from others
- ☐ Repeatedly rehearse a behavior

- ☐ Know exactly where support people are and how to reach them
- ☐ Have someone available to call "in case"
- ☐ Practice only with someone familiar
- ☐ Stay close to others
- ☐ Frequently visit doctors
- ☐ Stay near people

STABILITY
- ☐ Hold on to someone's hand or a cart
- ☐ Lean against a wall
- ☐ Sit instead of stand
- ☐ Stand or walk within reach of a wall or other support
- ☐ Tense up to keep control

LIMIT/RESTRICT PRACTICE
- ☐ Do something hurriedly
- ☐ Do something briefly
- ☐ Practice only when conditions allow you to feel confidant you can pull it off without anxiety
- ☐ Do activities only at certain times/certain days (i.e., avoid rush hours)
- ☐ Only practice when you are feeling well-rested and calm
- ☐ Avoid practicing if you are feeling poorly or weak
- ☐ Hope that the symptoms won't last much longer, that you will start feeling calmer soon
- ☐ Make "5 more minutes" bargains

DISTRACT YOURSELF
- ☐ Keep radio turned up
- ☐ Read a book
- ☐ Talk constantly
- ☐ Make your support person talk constantly
- ☐ Listen to music
- ☐ Meditate
- ☐ Close your eyes
- ☐ Look at the floor

☐ Sing songs to yourself
☐ Repeat "it's only anxiety"

LIMIT OR BLOCK SYMPTOMS
☐ Seek fresh air
☐ Roll down the window in the car
☐ Don't eat
☐ Don't exercise "too much"
☐ Stay in right hand lane
☐ Never pass a car
☐ Carry a "list of coping skills"
☐ Keep reading "list of coping skills"
☐ Block worried thoughts
☐ Wear loose or lightweight clothing
☐ Wear sunglasses
☐ Take an anti-anxiety pill "just in case"
☐ Drink alcohol
☐ Sip water
☐ Avoid caffeine

PROTECT FROM OTHERS
☐ Don't make eye contact
☐ Don't talk to people
☐ Wear high collar (so others can't see flushing on chest/neck)
☐ Practice with few people around
☐ Avoid crowds
☐ Avoid people

At first glance, it might be difficult to imagine what all these things have in common. People have used every strategy listed to avoid panic symptoms or the feared outcomes of panic. What unites these various tactics is that they are all based on the fundamental misperception that panic symptoms result in catastrophe. They are all attempts to prevent something that is not going to happen anyway, and they all interfere with recovery.

I am not suggesting that you instantly drop all these safety crutches. You will need to wean yourself from them gradually, through practice. In Step 6, you can use Chart 6 to help you pace those changes.

Now comes the final statement in your new self-help strategy. I have said that you need to get anxious on purpose, *encourage* the symptoms to continue for a long time, stop worrying and start supporting yourself, and let go of your safety crutches. Here is what comes next:

Do this over and over, in all your fearful situations. To overcome the drama of panic, you must practice your new skills again and again. You need to apply them in as many different locations and circumstances as possible. That process makes for solid learning.

Your New Self-Help Strategy

- Get anxious on purpose.
- Once you are anxious, *encourage* the symptoms to continue for a long time.
- During this time, stop worrying and start supporting yourself.
- And let go of your safety crutches.
- Do this over and over, in all your fearful situations.

STEP 5: Purposely Create Your Symptoms

You can begin to practice this self-help strategy now, in any way you choose. Or, you can wait, and continue with the next two steps first. If you are ready to practice in your feared situations now, experiment by going out into your world and getting anxious on purpose. Once you are anxious, encourage the symptoms to continue. During this time, stop worrying about how bad things might get and start reminding yourself that you can handle these physical sensations. Gradually eliminate your safety crutches, the behaviors that you think are protecting you from anxiety (such as, always sitting near the exit or never driving in the passing lane). Choose to get anxious over and over, in all your fearful situations. This approach will help you win over panic. You will discover, as thousands of others have, that panic simply cannot run roughshod over you when you face it directly.

Even if you are ready to apply these principles during your daily activities, it is important that you also learn through specific structured exercises. This way, you can assure yourself that you are mastering the essential skills needed to break the panic cycle. We are now going to target particular uncomfortable symptoms, to purposely generate those feelings, and teach you how to respond to them in a new way. You get to do this in a private setting, like your home, with no other intrusions, so you can concentrate only on these exercises.

Let's address the two central challenges of your recovery, your unconscious conditioning and your catastrophic fears. You are currently highly sensitive to some of these symptoms. In Step 5, you are going to learn how to be less sensitive. Your goal is to train yourself to have a non-anxious response to sensations that have been causing you to be anxious. This addresses your unconscious conditioning.

We will target four of the most common threats in panic disorder. These are:
- feeling detached from your body or surroundings
- fears related to your heart
- worries about your breathing
- feeling dizzy or faint

Through these exercises, we will also challenge your catastrophic predictions of what will happen if you have these sensations. These worries may include fears that you will faint, go crazy, or have a heart attack. You will learn that these uncomfortable sensations do not lead to such terrible outcomes.

During these exercises, you will briefly practice a task that provokes specific sensations. For example, breathing through a thin straw, which will cause you to have breathing difficulties or choking feelings. Or, spinning in a chair, to make you feel dizzy. Once you are experiencing these physical sensations, you will study them and rate your discomfort. We will start with practices that create mild to moderate anxiety and physical symptoms. We will then gradually work up to more threatening practices.

The exercises discussed in this section can create bodily sensations that are uncomfortable, but they are not dangerous in a physically healthy individual. As I mentioned before, a physician should evaluate everyone who experiences panic. Before proceeding with the steps outlined in this book, it is important to identify if you have any medical conditions for which treatment is required, or for which the exercises in this book would not be advisable.

Here are the sets of exercises you will be performing:

TABLE 7: PRACTICE CREATING SYMPTOMS

Type of Symptoms	Task	Instructions	Possible Symptoms
Detached Feelings	Stare at spot	Pick a spot on an empty wall and stare at it without moving your eyes.	Detachment from self, seeing spots, visual distortions
	Stare at light	Stare at a light for 30 seconds, then look at a blank wall.	
	Stare in mirror	Look at your face in the mirror. Choose one spot, such as the bridge of your nose, and remain gazing there, without moving your eyes.	
Heart Symptoms	Step-ups	Take one step up onto a stair, and immediately step down. Do this repeatedly at a fast rate (enough to get your heart racing). 1-2 minutes.	Heart racing, sweating
	Any brisk exercise	Walk up and down stairs, or use an aerobic exercise machine. 1-2 minutes.	
Breathing Symptoms	Breath holding	Take a deep breath and hold it. 30 seconds.	Shortness of breath, heart racing
	Breathe through straw	Breathe through a thin straw for one minute. Then 2 minutes. Don't allow air through your nose. (Slightly pinch your nostrils together if needed.)	Breathing difficulties, choking feelings

Dizziness	Roll head	Drop your chin down to your chest and roll your head to the right. When you get to your shoulder, move your head across to your left shoulder (don't roll toward your back), and continue rolling down to your chest. 1 minute.	Seeing spots, dizziness
	Shake head	Lower your head slightly and shake it from side to side for 30 seconds.	
	Head between knees	Place your head between your knees for 30 seconds then quickly lift your head to an upright position.	Seeing spots, dizziness, faintness
	Walk in circles	Walk around in a small circle, about 3 feet in diameter. (Do this near a wall, chair or couch in case you need to catch your balance.) 1 minute.	
	Spin standing up	Stand and turn around quickly (Do this near a wall, chair or couch in case you need to catch your balance). 1 minute.	
	Spin in chair	Spin yourself in a swivel chair. Have someone else spin you. Stand. Walk around. 1 minute.	
	Hyper-ventilate	Breathe deep and fast. Exhale with a lot of force. 1 minute.	

The exercises in this step will certainly be hard for you. They are for everyone. When I do them, they are difficult for me! You will need to commit to feeling uncomfortable over the short run. The good news is that we know from positive research results that these procedures, added to the others in this book, help people get better.

How to Practice
Set three major goals during practice. Research has shown that when you apply these three principles, then you train your body and mind to respond more calmly to your threatening situations, fearful thoughts and physical sensations. These three goals will be the same when you begin practicing in the settings that frighten you.
- Frequency – You must practice often enough.
- Intensity – You need to face the strong physical sensations that you are afraid of, not just the weak ones.
- Duration – During each practice, you must voluntarily and purposely encourage those uncomfortable sensations over an extended period, not briefly.

Here are some specific guidelines, including suggestions on frequency, intensity and duration.

Use a coach. It will be easier to conduct these exercises when someone helps you, just as a coach guides an athlete. If possible, ask a family member, a friend or your therapist to support you when you practice. This might include your coach doing an exercise before you do it, or doing it with you.
- Your coach is your cheerleader, and your motivator when you are feeling frightened. He/she encourages you to schedule your practices every day, and helps you stay on track when you want to procrastinate.
- If you are feeling too worried to start, your coach can demonstrate an exercise for you before you try it. Or, he/she can do the exercise with you. Eventually you should do the exercise alone.
- During the exercise, and during the first 30 seconds or so after stopping, your coach should say very little so that

you can concentrate on your task. Afterwards, he/she can ask you two questions:
- "What are you thinking right now?"
- "What are you feeling right now?"

And, he/she can encourage you in the following ways:
- "You can do it!" "Stay with it." "You're fine." "You can handle these feelings." "You are doing great!"
- After the exercise, your coach can help you think about how you felt and can support you in completing a rating form (Charts 2 and 3, later in this step). He/she can also ask you if you are doing anything to make yourself more comfortable during the practice. (As I will mention in a moment, your goal is to remove any safety crutches and feel your symptoms as strongly as possible.)

Purposely start practicing with your lowest state of anxiety and most modest symptoms. It will be easier for you to build your tolerance to stronger symptoms by starting with mild ones. There are several ways to do this:
- Scan through these lists and choose the ones that seem easiest to handle. Feel free to skip around within the different lists.
- If a certain practice seems intimidating to you, start by having your coach do it, then do it with your coach, then do it alone while your coach watches. Eventually you should do all exercises alone, to develop your coping skills and your confidence.
- You can also reduce the time of a practice to help you tolerate the sensations. In later sessions, you should return to the exercise to practice feeling the sensations to their fullest.
- If any particular exercise surprises you by generating intense anxiety, and you become more frightened than you want, then you can stop that practice and move to an easier one. (But, commit to returning to that exercise eventually.)

During each practice, your goal is to become as uncomfortable as possible by creating the strongest symptoms possible. After you have done several practices with low anxiety, start pushing yourself to go for the full experience, for as long as you can and as vigorously as you can tolerate. Efforts to be careful, or to try and control the symptoms, are safety crutches that I described in the last step. Ask yourself if you are doing anything to make yourself more comfortable during the practice. Work to let those behaviors go. Be reckless. Don't hold back. This is your laboratory and its purpose is to strengthen you to confidently face symptoms in the future.

After you end an exercise, stand still for at least 30 seconds to account for your thoughts and feelings. Some people feel most uncomfortable during the exercise, while others feel more distress in the moments after stopping. You may not notice a response until two to three minutes after you stop. Don't be surprised by a delayed reaction. That is quite common for some people.

If you are feeling anxious after you complete the practice session, you can take time to practice calming your body down. Refer to the breathing skills I described in Step 3. Sit quietly and take nice gentle Natural Breaths for a couple of minutes, or try a few Calming Breaths. As you quiet your thoughts and calm your breathing, you will begin to restore your body to its normal state.

Always chart your practices. In the charts, on pages 56 and 57, notice that there are two ratings for each practice. The first, "intensity of sensation," indicates how strong or uncomfortable you think the physical sensation is. Rate the intensity as either "low," "medium" or "high." The second rating, "level of fear," is how scared you feel in response to the sensation. Again, your choices are from "low" to "high." The charts help you with two goals. The first is to learn that there is a difference between how strong the sensation is and how frightened you become by it. Most people don't even think about the difference between the two during anxious times, but the distinction is important. For instance, at some amusement parks, there is a ride called "Round-up." Riders step into a large cylinder and stand up against the wall. The cylinder begins spinning, faster and faster, and then the floor of the cylinder drops away, leaving the riders suspended against the wall by centrifugal force. The sensations are quite intense while you are spinning! You can feel your body pressed against the wall, and you can barely lift your arm away from your side. Everyone feels that. How frightening the experience is will be different for each person. Some will feel excited and want to do it again, while others will be so scared that they refuse to do *any* more rides that day.

The same is true for your uncomfortable sensations. Your heart will beat strongly in one exercise, you will have difficulty taking a full breath in another, and you will feel quite dizzy in yet another. You will record those reactions in your "intensity of sensation" rating. In the "fear level" columns, you will rate how scared you became by those sensations.

The second goal is to get your fear rating down to "low," even if the intensity of your sensations remains high. Intense symptoms are absolutely uncomfortable. *Anyone who breathes through a cocktail straw for 60 seconds, or who is spun around in a chair for a minute, is going to feel physically uncomfortable.* Over time, however, you will learn not to feel overwhelmed when you notice the strong symptoms. You won't perceive the sensations as unbearable. You will accomplish this through repeated practice.

Begin by recording in Chart 2, which lists each of the four groups of sensations (detached feelings, heart, breathing, dizziness). Use Chart 2 to evaluate which practices may help you reduce your fear.
- If you practice an exercise twice for the suggested time and you have a low fear level each time, then you don't

need to practice that one again. Make sure, however, that you aren't controlling your anxiety by any safety crutches, like distracting your attention while you are looking in the mirror, or doing step-ups slowly.
- If you have a medium or high fear during an exercise, or if you end it early to keep in control of your feelings, then you should continue working with that exercise.

Once you have evaluated which exercises will be most helpful (the ones that give you at least "medium" fear, or the ones you stopped early), then start using Chart 3. Use this chart to continue practicing any tasks in Chart 2 that you did not master. These include any in which you had medium or high fear levels, those requiring safety crutches, or those you felt too anxious to finish.

Notice the new column in Chart 3, called, "Fearful and/or Supportive Thoughts." When you practice, record any fearful thoughts you had before you started, during the actual practice, and in the time immediately after you stop. Also, jot down any supportive thoughts you had ("I can handle this." "I'm going to stick it out till the end.")

Chart 2: Practice Creating Symptoms

Type of Symptom	Task	Suggested time	Actual time	Intensity of sensation*			Fear Level**		
				Low	Med	High	Low	Med	High
Detached Feelings	Stare at a spot	2 minutes							
	Stare at a light	30 seconds							
	Stare in the mirror	1 minute							
Heart Symptoms	Step-ups	1-2 minutes							
	Brisk exercise	1-2 minutes							
Breathing Symptoms	Hold breath	30 seconds							
	Straw breathing	1 minute							
Dizziness	Roll head	1 minute							
	Shake head	30 seconds							
	Head between knees	30 seconds							
	Walk in circles	1 minute							
	Spin standing up	1 minute							
	Spin in chair	1 minute							
	Hyper-ventilate	1 minute							

* How strong or uncomfortable physical sensation is.
** How scared you feel in response to the sensation.
Print out a full size version of this chart from the ADAA website at www.adaa.org.

Chart 3: Practice Creating Symptoms							
Date	Task	Time	Fearful and/or Supportive Thoughts	Intensity of sensation*			Fear level**		
				Low	Med	High	Low	Med	High

* How strong or uncomfortable physical sensation is.
** How scared you feel in response to the sensation.
Print out a full size version of this chart from the ADAA website at www.adaa.org.

Create a schedule to practice frequently. It is better to cluster your practices over several days instead of practicing once or twice over the course of several weeks.
- Practice approximately 30 minutes each time.
- It is OK to either focus on a single exercise each session or to practice several different ones.

An ambitious schedule is to practice five days a week, twice a day. A minimal schedule is once a day, four days out of seven.

Repeat each exercise a number of times over several days, until you only feel low fear. It is important to practice these exercises repeatedly, for three reasons.
- First, you will discover that your feared sensations are not signals of some horrible problem. You can produce them voluntarily, and then they go away.
- Second – and most important – you will learn that you can handle these symptoms. Remember the terms of our worry equation from the last step: you will worry about panic when you think it will be horrible and when you think you can't cope with it. These exercises will help you downgrade your "horrible" belief to "hard" or "uncomfortable," and they will help increase your belief in your ability to cope.
- Third, repeated practice will help your body and mind change their conditioned fear responses to the sensations.

Study your fearful and supportive thoughts. By studying your answers in Chart 3, you can keep track of how your thoughts influence your fear level. Notice whether your negative interpretations ("This is too much!") are associated with higher fear levels. Gradually work to introduce supportive comments, such as "I can handle this," or, "I can tolerate a lot more than I could before." Discover how these comments help you tolerate the intense sensations. Observe how, sometimes, even when you predict you can't handle a symptom, you handle it anyway. Maybe your predictions aren't so accurate!

STEP 6: Take Your Skills Out into Your World

Remember your basic strategy for winning over panic: **Get anxious on purpose.** Once you are anxious, *encourage* **the symptoms to continue for a long time. During this time, stop worrying and start supporting yourself. Let go of your safety crutches. Do this over and over, in all your fearful situations.**

In the last step, you practiced most of this approach by facing your symptoms directly. In completing that practice, you should have learned the following: if you get anxious on purpose, and stay with those feelings, your anxiety will eventually decrease, *especially* if you do nothing to reduce it.

In this step, I am adding two new sets of worries that threaten you: where you practice and the structure of the activity. In Step 5, location didn't matter. You could practice in the privacy of your own home and, when you did, you knew that the exercise would last less than 5 minutes. Now, you are going to practice in environments that seem threatening to you. These are places where you think that you might have anxiety or a panic attack. You are going to have less structure than you did with the exercises of Step 5. A practice may last for a period of time that you cannot fix in advance. You may not know how many people will be there. Simply put, you won't know exactly what will happen next. This typically makes people more anxious.

The easy part is that there are no new skills you need to learn in Step 6. You will use the exact same skills you used in Step 5. The only change is that these situations usually seem more threatening because people tend to worry more when they have less structure, or when they are in a location where they had trouble in the past. You may have thoughts similar to these: "I can't have a panic attack *there* (in the mall, at the restaurant, with friends, while standing in line!) That would be awful! I won't be able to cope!"

Remember the equation from Step 4 that we are learning to modify:

| **Worry about panic** | = | There is a good chance + I am going to get anxious | It's starting to + happen now | It could become a severe panic attack and that would be horrible! |

I can't cope with that! I'll fall apart!

If these new practices seem more threatening to you, it is for two reasons. You predict that the outcome of your anxiety or panic will be severe and horrible, and you predict that you can't cope with that.

To break the panic cycle, you only have to focus on these two predictions:

| **Choose to approach panic** | = | There is a good chance + I am going to get anxious | It's starting to + happen now | It could be a panic attack and that will be uncomfortable |
| | | | I will handle it | |

As you begin to enter these new situations, remember this: *if you choose to be anxious on purpose, it is just a matter of time before your anxiety will diminish.* You don't have to clutch onto someone's hand, or repeatedly tell yourself that you can escape whenever you want, or any of the dozens of other safety crutches (see Table 6, on page 43). Face your feared symptoms directly, without bracing yourself, and they will diminish. It is only a matter of time before the relaxation response sets in to counter the emergency sensations that trouble you as you become tense.

Planning for your practice
Start by creating a written set of your feared situations. Follow these instructions, writing down each of your answers.
1. Using Chart 4, list all of the events in which you have difficulty managing your anxiety and all the situations you avoid out of fear of panic.
2. After listing them, rank them from least difficult (#1) to most difficult (#10). Which do you predict will generate the lowest fear levels, and which will you cope with best? Those should be your lower numbers.

Chart 4: Listing & Ranking My Feared Situations			
Event	Rank*	Event	Rank

* #1 = least difficult.
Print out a full size version of this chart from the ADAA website at www.adaa.org.

3. Now, transfer the top ten situations, from easiest to hardest, to Chart 5. Don't allow the space limitations of this book to limit the number of items that you list on the printed charts. You should confront all the situations that curb your freedom. Add on to these lists using separate paper if you have more situations to deal with.

In the second column, describe what you are afraid might happen. Are you afraid people will see you acting anxious? That you won't be able to concentrate? That you will have a heart attack? Or, that you will have to pull off the highway?

In the last column, list the different safety crutches you might use in that situation. Refer back to Table 6 in Step 4. Will you hide your hands so no one can see them shake? Do you keep a list so you won't forget what you are planning to buy? Must you take your pulse? Do you repeatedly check the map for distances between exits?

Chart 5: Details of My Feared Situations		
Event	What I am afraid will happen	Safety crutches I commonly use here
#1.*		
#2.		
#3.		
#4.		
#5.		
#6.		
#7.		
#8.		
#9.		
#10.		

#1 = easiest.
Print out a full size version of this chart from the ADAA website at www.adaa.org.

Practicing your skills
There are several ways to practice:
- You can choose to practice those events on your list that are easiest to handle. This way you can gradually build your skills.
- There may be events on your list that you want to master now, even though they are harder (for example, you want

to start driving alone). If you are motivated to tackle a tougher situation, go ahead.
- There may be threatening events that are a necessary part of your day or week, like grocery shopping or an office meeting. You will be facing them anyway, so you might as well practice your skills while you are there.

Remember that you need to commit to each of the following goals as you practice:
- Frequency – You must practice often enough, every day if you can, but at least three times per week. Frequent exposure to the feared situations will condition your body and mind to a new response. They will learn to handle those situations without becoming alarmed. Don't wait until you have a scheduled activity to practice your skills. If you have no events coming up that allow you to practice frequently enough, then create situations specifically to practice. If, for example, you are working on driving to the grocery store, then drive there whether or not you need groceries.
- Intensity – You need to face the strong physical sensations that you are afraid of, not just the weak ones. When you feel ready, let yourself have panic attacks in any of these situations. Learn that you can cope with them, even though they are uncomfortable.
- Duration – In each practice, you must voluntarily and purposely encourage those uncomfortable sensations over an extended period. You can't just make them brief episodes. A 45- to 90-minute practice is a great goal. This will help you become used to the variety of feelings you will experience during that time. It will help your mind and body consistently practice ways to cope with moments of anxiety or tension.

Chart 6 will help guide you as you practice in each of the feared situations on your list. Make copies of it and fill it out before each practice session. Remember that a "practice" is anytime you commit to honing your skills. This includes all situations that you worry about. They can be part of your regularly scheduled week, or you can plan them specifically to practice your skills.

How to set up your practice. Look at the second column of the chart, "What I will practice." Each of these checkboxes represents a goal. The more of these you commit to, the stronger your practice. Here is the purpose of each of them:

- **Choose to get anxious on purpose** – This should be your goal for every practice. It is the cornerstone of your plan to break panic's hold on you. If you try *not* to get anxious, if you wish and hope that you won't get anxious, then panic has a lot of power over you. If you commit yourself to creating anxiety, then you begin to take control. So put a check by this one each time.
- **Stay anxious** – The goal is to stay uncomfortable for as long as possible. Don't just stay within the situation for an extended time. Try to keep the symptoms going for as long as possible. Wish for more symptoms! Hope for continued discomfort!
- **Encourage your symptoms to get stronger** – Here you are to go one step further by *wanting* your physical sensations to become more powerful. If you are afraid of your racing heart, then encourage your heart to beat *faster*. If you worry about dizziness, then try to feel *more* lightheaded.
- **Let go of worries about the consequences** – Do the best you can to not dread terrible things happening. Stop runaway fears that start out with, "What if…." ("What if they see me?" What if the symptoms get worse?") Stay in the present and remind yourself: "It's OK that I'm anxious right now." "I'll be fine no matter what I feel." "I'm scared, and I'm safe." "I can handle these symptoms."
- **Let go of your safety crutches** – These are from your list on Chart 5, "Details of my feared situations." Once you have successfully practiced getting anxious on purpose in one of your feared situations, then the next time it occurs, begin to change your safety crutches. For instance, if you always carry a cup of water with you when you go out, start leaving it in the car. If you usually make sure you are breathing calmly from your belly when you practice, then

start ignoring your breathing pattern. Set as your goal the removal of all your safety crutches from each of your feared situations. If you check this item, then list in the next column exactly how you will change your safety crutches.
- **Create physical sensations** – When you check this item, you agree to generate physical sensations on purpose – just as you did in Step 5 – while you are in the feared situation. So, if you are about to practice standing in line at the bank and tend to worry about your breathing, then decide to hold your breath for 30 seconds while you stand in line. If you are working on your fear of elevators, and you worry about feeling detached from your body, then stare at the light fixture while you ride up several floors. If you avoid physical exercise because you don't want your heart to race, then decide to climb the stairs quickly instead of taking the elevator. If you check "Create physical sensations," then identify what you will do in the column, "How I will create symptoms," using the Step 5 practice items.
- **Create fearful thoughts** – This is a new one, and therefore I want you to practice it after you have successfully practiced the other five on this list. Understanding this one will take some concentration, because it appears to contradict the practice above that says, "Let go of worries about consequences." I am not asking you to worry about how things could go wrong when you are experiencing an event. In fact, I want you to remember that things might be hard but not *horrible*, and that you can handle whatever happens. You learned this in Step 5, and now you will learn it as you continue to practice. However, your fearful thoughts are going to pop up anyway, whether you want them to or not. Your mind is conditioned to think those thoughts when you get close to your feared situation. For a while, they will come automatically whenever you enter a threatening situation, or even *think* about the activity.

Your job is to practice not getting scared by the thoughts. I want you purposely to call up your fearful thoughts, just like you call up your feared physical sensations. In your mind, make the statement or pose the question. Then let your body react to it. Either you will feel more anxious or you won't feel anything. That doesn't really matter. The important task is to purposely create the messages in your head instead of trying to block them. Blocking them is merely another kind of safety crutch.

For example, as you sit in the inside seat of a booth during a dinner with others, you might plan purposely to think, "I could have a panic attack right now and really embarrass myself in front of my friends." While you are driving, you could repeat one of your common fears, like, "I'm afraid I'll black out and smash into another car."

Here are the steps to take in practicing fearful thoughts:
1. Decide to practice this skill and check it off on Chart 6.
2. Write down on the chart the statements or questions you will practice.
3. During the event, mentally call up one of the thoughts on purpose.
4. If the thought makes you anxious, let your body respond, and encourage any physical sensations.
5. After a few minutes, when your body has quieted down again, you can call up the thought again.
6. Continue practicing this skill in future events until you have achieved a low fear response to the thoughts.

Chart 6: Preparing to Practice*		
Event:	Date:	Length of practice:
What I will practice:	How I will change safety crutches:	
☐ choose to get anxious on purpose ☐ encourage symptoms to get stronger ☐ stay anxious ☐ let go of worries about consequences ☐ let go of safety crutches ☐ create physical sensations ☐ repeat fearful thoughts	How I will create symptoms:	
	Fearful thoughts I will repeat:	

* Make copies of this chart.
 Print out a full size version of this chart from the ADAA website at www.adaa.org.

As you begin your practice, you can work on several fearful situations during the same week. In general, start with less threatening practices and work your way up to harder ones. Remember that most of our lives are not mapped out for our convenience. You will probably have to skip around on your list simply because your daily routine brings you into contact with different events. For example, you might want first to talk on the telephone with someone who intimidates you before you have to talk to them in person. They also may just walk up to you at the parking lot and begin talking.

What to do if your physical sensations or worries become too uncomfortable for you
When the symptoms get stronger, your first line of defense should be to invite them to continue. Make your best effort to stand there and say, "Come on panic, give me your best shot." As you first start facing strong panic symptoms this sounds like quite a bad idea. "What if it *does* give me its best shot!?" Even though you are scared, try it. You may be quite surprised even within one or two minutes. When you fully experience panic, even strong panic – and you don't fight it – it tends to diminish on its own.

Sometimes, though, you may feel so uncomfortable or worried that you want to stop the symptoms. It is always OK to find a safety crutch if you become overwhelmed. That's what crutches are for, to help you heal. If you need to lean on a crutch to get out of a difficult situation, then do so. Come back another day to begin again. Ask yourself, "What can I do to support myself right now?" Along with your favorite crutches, you can choose any one or more of the following options:

- You can take a few Calming Breaths and relax your body.
- You can involve yourself more actively in your surroundings. Seek out a conversation or find something in your environment to study carefully.

- You can tell a supportive person about what you are feeling and what you want to do to take care of yourself. You can let that person support your efforts.
- You can leave the situation for a brief period as a way to increase your comfort and control, then return and continue your practice.
- You can leave the situation and not return at this time. As you continue to practice your skills, over time you will learn to remain in the scene.

After the Practice

When you finish a practice, use Chart 7 to compare your predictions about what terrible things would happen (as in Chart 5) and what actually happened. Was it really as bad as you thought? Did you make a fool of yourself? Faint? Have a heart attack? And if things did turn out better than expected, what actions did you take to influence this result? Did you let yourself be anxious or have a panic attack? Did you stay in the scene even though you wanted to leave? Did you let go of a safety crutch or two?

Chart 7: Learning from Practice				
Date	Event	What I was afraid would happen	What actually happened	How I influenced that outcome

Print out a full size version of this chart from the ADAA website at www.adaa.org.

Take a look at the worry equation again.

Worry = How likely is it to happen? + How soon will it happen? + How bad will it be?
How will I cope with it?

We have been working on all four of these components to reduce the amount you worry before, during and after an anxiety-provoking event. Here is the approach I have been encouraging you to take:

- How likely is it (my anxiety or panic) to happen? It is highly likely because I am *trying* to make it happen. I *want* it to happen. It's OK.
- How soon will it happen? It will happen very soon because I am purposely doing a practice now to *make* it happen. It's OK for it to happen soon.
- How bad will it be? This is the part we are working on now. As you practice in your natural environment, continue to study the difference between what you predict will happen and what happens. That study will help you lessen the severity of your assessment, from "It will be awful, horrible!" to "It will be tough or hard."
- How will I cope? This is the other part we are currently working on. The third column of Chart 7 addresses that question. "How I influenced that outcome" will remind you of your coping skills. These will often be to wait out the symptoms, to try to make them stronger and to reassure yourself that you can handle them until they pass.

As you continue your practice, remember why you are seeking these stances in the face of panic. Here is how we are changing that worry equation over time:

Choose to approach = There is a good chance I am going to get anxious + It's starting to happen now + It could be a panic attack and that will be uncomfortable

I will handle it

69

This is the equation that you should use to recover from panic attacks. However you practice, and whatever techniques you use, the efforts should reflect this model. If you practice frequently enough and long enough using this model, you will be surprisingly pleased with the results.

Step 7: Now, Greet Panic in Your Daily Life

In Steps 4, 5 and 6, you studied how to provoke panic by encouraging and even trying to intensify your uncomfortable symptoms. I encourage you to take several weeks to practice these skills.

Once you finish your weeks of practice, how should you manage the panic that rises up in your day? There are three ways that you can respond to panic, resist it, permit it or provoke it. Your goal is to stop resisting it and start permitting it or provoking it. I will show you how in this step.

Stop resisting panic
You are quite familiar with resisting panic, since that is our instinctual response to fearful situations. When you resist panic, you give strong and rigid messages to yourself. They tend to start with opening phrases such as, "I can't...." Examples of these expressions abound. Do any of these sound familiar?

"I can't tell anyone."
"I can't let anyone see me be anxious."
"I can't make a mistake."
"I can't let myself feel any anxiety."
"I can't let these symptoms increase."
"I can't handle these symptoms."
"I can't have a panic attack."
"I can't take the risk."

Imagine the gentleman in the drawing attempting to introduce himself to a friend or colleague. He expends so much mental energy frightening himself, it is no wonder that he feels scared. If you put this many expectations and restrictions on yourself, you are more likely to want to retreat, to avoid, or to run away.

Choice 1: Permit the symptoms

When you permit panic, you take back control of the situation. No longer are you controlled by where you are, whom you are with, how you are performing or how you are feeling. Your instructions to yourself tend to begin with the phrases "I can…" or "It's OK…." Here are some examples:
"It's OK to take a chance here. This is a place to practice my skills."
"It's OK if they see my hands shake."
"I can be anxious and still perform my task."
"I can handle these symptoms."
"It's OK to feel safe here."
"I can make mistakes and still be OK."
"I can slow down and think."
"I can trust my body."
"I can stay here or I can leave."

One of the central fears of panic is to feel trapped or out-of-control. Any messages that limit your options ("I can't let myself get more anxious.") will also increase your discomfort. When you permit yourself to have a variety of responses ("It will be OK whether I'm relaxed or uptight. I can handle being nervous."), then you won't feel so trapped and won't get as anxious.

Imagine that you are about to enter a restaurant, and in the past you have left this same restaurant because of anxiety. What will you do if your attitude is, "Once I order my meal, I can't leave. I would be humiliated if anyone saw me get up and walk out"? Most likely you would begin to feel the apprehension and pressure to perform this task perfectly. You would watch for any internal signals telling you that you might not be able to handle it. If you did notice a few small symptoms, you might be more likely to say, "I can't do this today." Reducing your options will reduce your chances of success.

What if, instead, you said any of these? "If I need to, I can get up and leave. It's really no big deal. If I've already ordered, I'll just leave $10 on the table as I go. Nobody else really cares." With this attitude, you will feel much more comfortable about entering the restaurant. This is because the greater sense we have that we can comfortably escape someplace, the easier it will be for us to enter. The more you develop an attitude that permits you to have freedom of choice, the more you will be able to make healthy choices.

Here are some other permissive messages you can offer yourself:

> "I don't have to let these feelings stop me."
> "I always have options, no matter what."
> "This is not an emergency. I can think about what I need."
> "I can trust my body."

"As I learn to trust my body, I will have even more control of my body."
"It's OK to say no to others."
"I don't have to be perfect to be loved."
"Everything is practice. I don't have to test myself."
"I deserve to feel comfortable here."

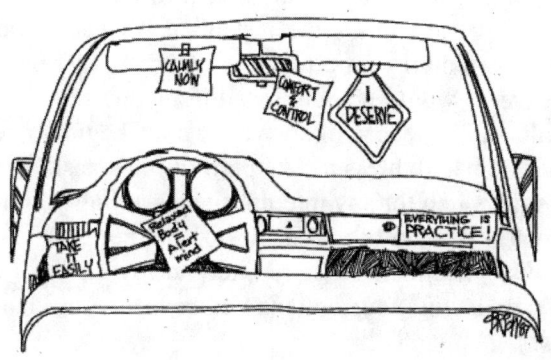

How to Permit Your Symptoms

Here is a simple four-step procedure to use when you face a panicky situation. First, notice that you are working yourself up by your worried thoughts ("What if the symptoms get overwhelming!?"). Choose to let those thoughts go. Your task is to stop focusing on your worries.

Second, remind yourself that you can handle your symptoms by accepting them and waiting them out. Use any of the other permissive messages in this section ("I can…" "It's OK…") to support your efforts.

Third, use your breathing skills to help you let go of those worried thoughts and begin to quiet your body and mind down. Take two or three Calming Breaths or begin Natural Breathing. This important step accomplishes two tasks. By focusing on your formal breathing skills, you pull your attention away from your fearful thoughts and you help your body calm down at the same time.

Choice 1: Permit Your Symptoms

1. Notice your worried thoughts and choose to stop them. ("These thoughts aren't helpful. I can let them go.")
2. Notice your uncomfortable physical symptoms and choose to accept them. ("It's OK that I'm anxious right now. I can handle these feelings.")
3. Take two or three pleasant Calming Breaths or begin gentle Natural Breaths.
4. Stay in the situation while you continue to let go of your fearful thoughts and accept your physical discomfort.

Fourth, do the best you can to stay in the situation instead of escaping. Expect to cycle through the first two steps again and again as you wait out the symptoms. You will be afraid, let those thoughts go, then accept your uncomfortable symptoms.

As you practice using your positive, supportive comments, don't expect that they will instantly cancel out your fearful, negative thoughts. You will continue to hear your worried thoughts. When you hear them, take the time to reconsider their message and offer yourself another, more positive choice. Moments later, you may hear yet another fearful thought. Again, offer yourself a choice to that worry. The drawing below illustrates this process.

Choice 2: Provoke Your Symptoms

Provoking your symptoms is similar to what you were doing in Step 6. When you notice anxiety begin to grow toward panic, decide to provoke the symptoms. Start by taking a Calming Breath and beginning Natural Breathing. Don't fight your symptoms or run away. Then identify your most uncomfortable symptom and try to increase it, through your willpower and instruction ("I want my face to become even more hot and red."). Once you have encouraged that symptom for a few moments, start on all your other uncomfortable sensations. Try to will them to get stronger, too. Stay with your effort while you breathe gently into your abdomen.

Choice 2: Provoke Your Symptoms

1. Take a Calming Breath and then begin Natural Breathing. Don't fight your physical symptoms and don't run away.
2. Observe your most uncomfortable physical symptom at this moment.
3. Encourage that symptom to get stronger ("Come on, heart, beat faster!").
4. Now attempt to increase all the other symptoms you notice. Examples: try to perspire more, become even dizzier, and make your legs feel like jelly, right now.
5. Continue Natural Breathing, while you consciously and fully attempt to increase all your symptoms of panic. Do not get trapped in worried, critical, or hopeless comments. ("This better start working soon! I certainly must be doing this wrong. It will never work.")

If you have any trouble applying this technique of provoking your symptoms, look first at your attitude. You need to have a complete willingness to embrace the symptoms in order to diminish their power. You can't secretly wish that your symptoms won't get stronger. You need to mean it when you say, "Come on, heart, beat stronger." By consciously resisting your heart's tendency to beat stronger you are, in fact, causing it to do just that by telling your body to be on guard for something dangerous. Honestly and consciously encouraging it to beat stronger will serve as a message to your unconscious. It says that you are willing to get out of the way and let your own unconscious mind learn to master panic on its own. To conquer panic, you must stop resisting. Provoking is the very best way to stop resisting.

Some Final Words

> To dry one's eyes and laugh at a fall,
> And baffled, get up and begin again.
> —Robert Browning, *Life in a Love*

There are no absolute formulas to follow, rigidly, in order to conquer panic. These steps represent a general approach. They are a synthesis of work done by many dedicated researchers, psychiatrists, psychologists, social workers and counselors. They reflect the successes of thousands of people who have learned to break the cycle of panic.

The process of healing does not always follow a simple path, where one positive step forward follows another. Some people move smoothly ahead once they catch on to the techniques. Some take much longer and require professional guidance along the way. Most say that they progressed nicely for a while and then had a setback or two, which surprised and discouraged them.

We now know that setbacks are a natural part of recovery. After ruling out any physical illness, there are three possible reasons why they occur. First, the amount of stress in your life has increased, and you are expressing your anxiety through panicky symptoms. During these times, you may slip back into a pattern of fearful, doubtful thinking, which will make you more vulnerable to anxious feelings. Second, some people may cycle through periods of panic simply because of their biological makeup. Or, third, recovering from panic disorder or agoraphobia sometimes means that we have to face other uncomfortable changes in our lives, such as, becoming more assertive and independent in social relationships. Our unconscious can resist those adjustments by causing us to feel trapped by panic again.

What do you do when you have a setback? You do what worked before. Go back to your basic skills and practice approaching your goals through small steps. If you feel that you are lacking the internal strength and optimism to encourage yourself, turn to others in your community for reassurance. You may also have to re-evaluate your relationships with some of the people in your life to make certain you are maintaining your self-esteem and sense of worth. Panic is sometimes a warning flag that we are ignoring our important personal needs.

Some of you will read this book, diligently follow its guidelines and yet still make little headway against your panic attacks. Don't consider yourself a failure if you cannot break through this impasse alone. Instead, seek out a mental health professional that specializes in treating panic-related problems. This individual will know how to combine these self-help skills within a professional treatment program.

Other people will experience an *increase* in anxiety when they repeatedly face anxiety-provoking situations, even when they use these principles. If you think you are becoming more anxious over time instead of less anxious, this is also a reason to consult with a mental health professional who specializes in the treatment of anxiety.

Remember that you are successful every time you *decide* to practice, regardless of how long you are able to maintain and carry on with that commitment. Facing panic is not a test of your ability to stop all sensations of discomfort. Nor is it a test of your progress. This, and every other thing you do, is an opportunity to practice your ability to support yourself. The more you practice supporting *every* effort and attempt, the stronger you will become and the more willing you will be to practice.

Listen for any harsh self-criticisms or discouraging thoughts after your practice. "I *still* get anxious. What's wrong with me?! I'll never get better." Replace them with statements of support. "I'm working to change a lot of complex processes. I can't do it all at once, and I'm not trying to do it perfectly. One step at a time. I'm going to get there."

As you begin to work with the steps in this book and start your practice, be encouraged by the fact that we humans *can* take direct action to improve the quality of our lives. All of us deserve to look forward to a long and healthy future, to live our lives based on our values, our convictions, our excitement and our love of freedom. As adults, we choose to take risks in order to win these qualities. Once we attain them, we know that they were worth all of our struggles. Helen Keller's ability to overcome her limits is reflected in her basic attitude, which can remind you of the power of the human spirit:

Security is mostly a superstition. It does not exist in nature, nor do the children of men as a whole experience it. Avoiding danger is no safer in the long run than outright exposure. Life is either a daring adventure or nothing.